JACQUELINE SPRING is the pseudonym chosen by the author, who was born in 1946. She grew up in Glasgow, Scotland, the youngest of a large family of seven children. On leaving school, she worked as a nursery assistant, and then in libraries, before training as a primary teacher. After a few years at home with her first two children, she taught for some years before her third child, a little girl, was born. She now has her home in Scotland with her husband and four children.

Cry Hard and Swim was written in the midst of three experiences: that of being healed from a hurtful childhood, in a humane and professional way; that of being one of an incest survivors' group; and that of becoming involved with professional workers wanting to learn about helping incest victims. These three factors gradually came together to focus her attention on the need not only to write her own experiences of childhood, but also to go on to recall the details of her healing, for both survivors and concerned workers.

CRY HARD AND SWIM

The Story of an Incest Survivor

JACQUELINE SPRING

Published by VIRAGO PRESS Limited 1987
41 William IV Street, London WC2N 4DB
Copyright © Jacqueline Spring 1987
All rights reserved

British Library Cataloguing in Publication Data
Spring, Jacqueline
  Cry hard and swim : the story of an incest
  survivor.
  1. Incest   2. Fathers and daughters
  I. Title
  306.7'77   HQ71

  ISBN 0-86068-813-5

Typeset by Florencetype Ltd of Kewstoke, Avon

Printed in Great Britain by Cox & Wyman Ltd
of Reading, Berkshire

Contents

Acknowledgements

Throughout the writing of this book, I have been sustained by a great deal of emotional support, encouragement, constructive criticism and affection. For these, and much more, I would like to thank Olive Thomson, Kathy Kerr and 'Eve', who enabled me to begin.

For sharing, and giving me permission to use some of the material in 'Surviving Together', my sincere thanks go to the women in the Incest Survivors' Groups of the RSSPCC, Glasgow, and the Rape Crisis Centres, Glasgow and Edinburgh.

Finally, I thank with all my heart my very dear husband and children, who have shared (and survived!) so much of the journey.

Foreword

The art of the painter lies in allowing what is invisible to speak through the visible. In making the inner reality emerge through an outer reality, which is transparent to the eyes of the artist.

And this, too, is the art of the therapist. Yet the corresponding skill lies also in preserving that outer reality, the adult, while creating the conditions in which the inner child can uncurl from its defensive position and speak.

To arouse the hurt child within a person is relatively easy, given sufficient time and sympathy. The preservation of the adult wherein the child dwells is not so easy, for once the child does uncurl, it not only speaks, but yells and rages, screams and weeps, yearns for a different childhood, and despairs to discover that this can never be, that no one can ever take the place of the mother or father, and that this is the hard reality that has to be faced.

The adult is shaken by this inner storm, and only the consistent strength of respect provided by the therapist can hold the integrity of the person intact. For the energy aroused in the protesting child must by balanced by a complementary energy in the adult, an energy of new pride in adulthood. It is these opposing energies which achieve that eventual state of stillness in the self which is the source of all energy.

The ability to bring this about is what distinguishes the therapist as an artist, an artist with a profound concern for composition, the composition of the human being. And just as the artist gives vibrancy and purpose to the painting through the communication of faith, so the therapist can lift the despair of the child to joy by infusing the whole person with confidence, a confidence ranging through minute daily actions, and passing into a new attitude to life and to the self.

This book, written over almost three years, is an attempt to make sense of my experience of childhood and therapy, primarily for myself, secondarily for others. I am not attempting to promote any particular ideology or method. My deepest motivation in writing each sentence was to discover first exactly what it was that hurt me, and then exactly what it was that healed me. The contemplation of each assisted and reflected the contemplation of the other, and led into a truth that transcended both. It was not a new truth, but one which had been maturing in my mind through slow years, until at last it acquired a meaning in my own terms, and was born through my own poetry, a poetry constructed from my mother's torrent of music, and my father's avalanche of words.

PART 1

Child

Dearest Mama,

Is the very first word a lie? I don't know. But I know if I don't use that word you'll be 'hurt' — so there you have me.

I sometimes rest on my bed with the house in peace, everyone out. Someone has by chance left the radio on in another room. There is piano music playing softly in the distance, the sunlight slants in at a certain angle. Only two or three times have I accidentally found myself in this situation, but on each occasion the moment has, all at once, become timeless. My body floats, leaving only my mind, within which an immense stream of sweetness suddenly circulates. I just lie quiet, being a baby again in my cradle. The music tells me you are somewhere in the house, though far off. You will not come, but you are here.

Now I am looking directly into a blue clouded sky against which apple boughs are waving. You believe in putting babies under the trees because it keeps them happy longer. Keeps you happy longer, you mean. I don't know where the pain is, it is just all over me. Everywhere. There is a terrible noise going on, like ten jet aeroplanes flying low. I have been making the noise, feeling the pain, for ever and ever, with the hateful indifferent branches waving cheerfully into my pram.

Finally I am too exhausted with rage and pain to cry any more. A figure appears but it isn't you. It is Mina, one of our maids, who has six kids of her own and varicose veins. She walks a mile each way to and from the slums for the privilege of working long hours for you. You pay her above average so she has to keep coming, which saves you the bother of changing maids. She is tired and dull and rough with me. I am banged against her shoulder, winded with one push. I am brought into the house, and handed to Con to feed. Where are you?

Of course, I have already served my purpose. Which was to prove to your husband's tart that He still wanted you sexually, even after her. You met her in Copland's for afternoon tea, wearing your hat, and your spotless white gloves

3

and your eight-month bulge, expressly for the purpose of showing her that she had really made no difference at all to Him. That she was nothing.

You are very clever at putting over that message, but oh so stupid to want to. Even from your own point of view you have missed so much by not loving me. Because I am a beautiful baby. I am soft and cuddly, and I try so hard to be good for you. I love you so much. Too rarely you do appear. And when you ever do hold me, I am in ecstasy, gazing into your magical eyes. You sing to me. I go very quiet, enchanted, listening to the music with my entire being, body, brain, toes, guts. It comes not only from your voice, but vibrates through your soft inner arms, through your breast against which you hold me, but never enough. You did give me music, Mama. I have to thank you for that.

I have been fed. But I am still hungry. Con, who is eleven, burps me and puts me into the big black cot with bars. The door shuts.

My sadness is pressing all round, missing your cool touch. I still miss it, but do not want it from you now. You are alive but dead. You are the nothing who still puts me through the agony of seeking for the mother in other women, the agony of yearning for what can never be.

I am going to make you suffer, Mama. I am going to return again and again to show you all the love you could have had, and now will never have. And when eventually you do understand it, wait for it, hunger for it, I am going to abandon you too. You are going to end up knowing what you have lost, and what it is to be really hurt.

Grown Up

My parents
bound back to back
and perched
on kitchen chairs

4

at precarious angles
far found
within my brain
grin
through their strangling gags
when they hear me tell myself
I'm a big girl
now.

Dearest Mama,

I can count to seven. I walk down the black stone staircase counting the angels on the Christmas frieze. There are seven of them, one for each of us children. Large paper angels on a bright scarlet background. I wonder which of us made them? I wonder which of us painted the sixth, the second from the last one, grey?

I am the last angel, and I am white, so I can laugh at the family joke against David with the rest of them.

David, David. He is so utterly vulnerable. I half understand, tease him, torment him. Afterwards he comes and sits besides me and says, 'Let's be friends!' And very simply, we are again. He is the most beautiful person I have ever seen. Big brown eyes, elfin features, an enchanting smile. Totally unprepared for Him every time. David never seems to learn to dodge, to avoid destruction. And so, with your silent consent, he is slowly destroyed. Everyone sees it going on, no one questions the process. Gradually the machinery of his feelings begins to clank ominously, begins to grind down. Very secretly I know, but refuse to know. It is just too big a problem for me. So I retreat, telling myself that he no longer wants to be friends.

I am hiding. I used to hide behind your skirts, Mama, but you are not one of the safe hiding places. Not since the day you used the threat of Him against me, and I went reeling round the room with the shock of what that meant. In that moment, I lost you too.

I hide behind the sycamore tree at the far end of the garden, picking the bark off and watching the little bugs underneath scuttling about frantically, like the thoughts in my head. In the house there is more roaring and crying going on. I am afraid to be sent away too.

What does it mean, Mama, the word 'whore'? What did He mean when He lined us all up, the six angels who were left, eldest to youngest, and spoke so seriously for so long? What has Con done, that she is gone? Is sixteen too young to be engaged? But old enough to leave home, old enough to live in the cold world with no family. I think of the shouting, the warnings, the tears, the ultimatums, the last time she came down the stairs lugging the heavy suitcase, the silhouette of the young man waiting for her outside the frosted glass of the front door. She will never come back. We must never speak her name again.

But I do. I whisper it to myself, wandering from room to room, each one so big, so empty without her.

It is impossible to guess from your face what you are thinking, Mama. I dare not question you. To you, He is always right. There is always a good reason behind what He does. You love Him best, therefore His power is absolute. Of course we love Him too, and we know He is right. Which means it is we who are wrong, who are bad. We are all grey angels, pretending desperately to be white.

Family

We wave goodbye.
The jeep leaps over the dry and stony land.
Dad's at the wheel,
his foot makes the engine roar,
drowns the sound of weeping in the rear.
He stored up bread and water
but his fear
made the map route crumple in his head.

Sons and daughters humped together
hobnobbing like shorn sheep.
They have been duly warned.
They must not search the lowering sky
nor look out over the land.
Their job is to understand
where they are going.

Someone lurks behind the standing stone
that marks the landscape,
but he can't escape the jeep.
Hurt mind, he isn't planned for.
And so we grind him to a dead-
slow creep-crawling in the sand-
fly brother. My brother
I regret we must leave you behind,
we are too set to understand.

We look back.
He grows small long range.
See him scrawl
'All change for the Family'
on the strange stone . . .
grave?
He stands and waves goodbye.

Dearest Mama,
You never really forgave Him, did you? It broke the bubble
that you called 'my love for Him' to find Him in bed with
someone else. I am sorry for you. You have made sure of
that. I am also sorry for you quite on my own, to see you
quite on your own. Impossible to share this with anyone.
Better to forget it ever happened. But that is impossible
too.
    I see you smoothly moving through my childhood.
Bending to kiss me before going out in your pretty rain-
bow-coloured ballgown, scented, powdered, unfamiliarly

7

glamorous. Leading me quietly out of the music room when I won't behave. Baking peacefully in the sunny wooden kitchen. Making beds, eternally mending, addressing the maids in your calm, even tone. And always your music pervading the atmosphere, your improvisation of harmony. Everyone adores you. You are the rightful queen of the house. You never for a moment raise your voice in anger or protest. You never raise your hand.

He gives you this 'queen of the house' image. You accept it gratefully. It is one way to stay sane. Regain some dignity. You stay safely dead behind the facade. You do not want to find any more women in His bed. He does not want you to catch Him out again. It suits you both that I am available.

Do you know, Mama? I am never sure. It is unthinkable. I am just His little girl. He is my Daddy. We love each other. We are never challenged. No one, not even you, especially you, would dare. I myself don't dare to take the centre of the story, the meaning, and tear it out for myself, like twisting the stone free from a sweet plum. He alone knows for sure.

He is a man of great passion. His fury scares me, unpredictable, severely sarcastic, physically frightening. He is passionately religious too. An intellectual Catholic, He can verbally rip other religions to shreds. I see Him walking some hapless Jehovah's Witness round our oval front lawn for hours. The man departs, totally destroyed. He comes in to relate His victory, to our applause.

You applaud too, Mama. You do not identify with this random fellow-victim. You are elegantly isolated, afraid to make the effort to think, to feel. You abandon me to Him, knowing I have to come when He calls.

It is early morning, and He is calling. I am asleep. I will be asleep, no matter what. The others are not going to go. But He is calling. I steal from my sister's bed, where I have crept during the night. Crossing the landing, I enter the bedroom. He is looking at me, smiling. He pats the sheet

8

beside Him, which is turned down at the corner. I know what this means. My eyes are intent upon His, heart leaping. I step on a tightrope, leading from me to Him. He is pulling me with His eyes. The room starts to pulsate with my frightened heartbeats. One small foot placed slowly, carefully in front of the other. Not looking down at the abyss, eyes ahead, fixed on the sheet turned down. All effort put into not falling, behaving as if this were normal. But suddenly my foot slips and I do fall into His bed. He demands that I kiss his lips, and I give Him the vile kiss, pretending that it is a child's. But He will not let me pretend. With Him there is no pretence at all.

Where are you, Mama? You are downstairs doing the motherly things, clearing dishes, washing up, drying cups. Instead of upstairs doing the wifely things I am doing for you.

Child

Hat
by the river
left
where the child flung it
when she ran
from watching the dark skin
of water
where beetles worked
and swam.

River
of blood
from the child
as she flies
thudding to the stone
and lies
spreadeagled underneath
the climbing frame.

9

Dearest Mama,

Once again you have put me away from you. Put me with someone in pain. My job is to make them feel better for awhile. You are lending me out as if I were some precious possession of yours, some small seed of life to be placed in different soils, then uprooted and replanted somewhere else. It is taking me ages longer than it should to grow.

Something very serious has happened. This time, His crime cannot be concealed. Everyone knows but me, to whom, of course, no one explains. But the household is stricken, and nothing is the same. Suddenly you are 'worried'. This 'worry' is the reason for nothing being the same, and is accompanied by a sudden consciousness that, due to some catastrophe, far from being comfortably off, we are wretchedly poor. There is a queer flavour about our poverty. It is not romantic poverty, as in stories I have read. No bread and water, no rags. No signs at all, except that you say you are worried. We still have perfect food, abundantly served on Wedgwood, silver, linen, lace. There are still expensively fragrant soaps in the bathroom. You are not very good at being poor, Mama.

On the other hand, you are good at being loyal. You take me aside one day, sit me down, and exclaim very fiercely, 'If anyone says your father is a thief, it isn't true! Your father is a very sick man.' Too true. I could have told you that years ago, Mama, had you been able to hear. But you don't explain any further, just leave me filled with your fear, only with nothing for it to bite on.

So here we are, groping in a fog of anxiety within our large stone property. However, I emerge to run, barefoot, unwashed, dressed in shorts in order to be as free as possible to follow my fantasies all day. You never notice I go barefoot every day of my tenth summer. Shoes are necessary only for church. I walk miles along the pavements of suburbia, taking great pride in my hardening footsoles. You are too lost in your own troubles to see.

It is my happiest summer. For now I can feel a delicious

10

contempt for Him. Slobbering around the house, weeping at a moment's notice, wetting Himself. His tempers are now merely despicable. Whenever He enters a room, I leave it, knowing I am hurting Him, but unable to stand His presence. I am told that a gradual disintegration will take place.

Yet it takes me a long time to accept that He is ill. This is some new trick, designed to humiliate us all further. An excuse for His crime. Slowly my distrust of this new aspect of Him starts to dissolve. Gradually, and in small bursts, relief takes over. He is really going to die, at last. I have to keep a solemn face while being told this, but it is everything that I want, really. I so look forward to Him not existing. To being only your child. I have to protect you from my horrifying thoughts. You must never know.

But somehow, you do. From then on, I am sent to one relative after another, to be kept out of your way during the holidays. It is always presented to me as a special treat.

I am aware dimly of the pain of these relatives. Aunt Kate, childless and alcoholic. A bleak farmstead, where I develop a nervous stammer, by which she is puzzled, angered, and finally sadistically amused. Aunt Anne, your sister. Ugly, immensely rich, possessed by a cold man who is unattainable. It is kept very dark. Especially in your mind, so that you don't think twice about sending me there. I am stuffed with the haute cuisine she is obsessed with, dressed like a doll in new, fashionable clothes, permitted to listen to a series of smart witticisms between adults, which pass for conversation. I am fooled by the talk. I think I know how adults really want me to be, instead of so tiresomely childish. I strive very hard to please. She is amused by this, helps me on with a little 'advice'. Her generosity, her disillusion, her worldliness, her world-weariness, combine to educate me in confusion. I sit in a richness of gifts, colours, Christmas scents, silks, brocades, drawing her by the fire. It is my first real, unstylised drawing, and I am so proud of it. She is deeply and truly sad when she looks at it, and I suddenly realise why.

But I still look down on you when I return, Mama. You are not as knowledgeable as I. You don't have the polish of your sister. For the first time I am bitterly ashamed of you. And of myself, for feeling so.

Mother

She rains upon me
pouring down relentlessly
and I am soaked through.

I come inside
not to catch cold
and remembering she recommended
having a hot bath
I won't.

I'll have a shower instead
strip off and shut tight
the wetproof curtains.

The shower begins
pouring down relentlessly
and I am soaked through
her tears.

Dearest Mama,
I am so lonely for you. Your absence itself is a constant presence, clamouring through the thoughts behind my everyday conversations.

There now, are you satisfied? Yes. It really pleases you to know that I miss you so much it is painful. My pain is your pleasure. Now, only now, are you certain you are loved. But you don't really want me with you. My presence disturbs you, accuses you. You retreat into echoes and excuses.

I am thirteen and in love. There is no doubt in my mind that I have found the perfect person to belong to. My conversation is filled with this person. I simply cannot stop talking, but do, abruptly one day, when I suddenly see a contemptuously amused look on your face. My teacher is quickly put into secret files in my brain. I am still in love, but now acutely aware of the necessity to protect my heart. Unfortunately I cannot protect it from her. It takes her a year to tire of, and dismiss me, and I have to return to you. Once again, you send me away.

This time, I really enjoy the holidays. This time I am saved from pain and rejection. For it is Con you have sent me to, and she welcomes and accepts me, just as I am. We have long talks, sometimes lasting all night. I learn that my femininity is a valuable commodity, much desired. I feel like a poor man, newly told he has a room full of treasure in his house, to which he has no key.

Con surrounds herself with 'lame ducks', people with tragic lives like her own. I meet them, hear all their stories, and am immensely moved by them. By being accepted so totally, I learn to accept the abnormal too, but not to discriminate. I discover how vast, complicated and frightening life can be for others also, like huge storm waves scattering and smashing small boats.

But even though Con is pointing this out when she talks about these others to me, there is something about her that also reassures. She is full of vitality and irrepressible fun. When she listens, she fixes her eyes attentively on mine. When she speaks, it is as if she has heard what I have not dared say, and answers it. And when she answers it, it is as if I have permission to be.

She has an intolerance of authoritarianism, humbug, pomposity. At thirteen, this suits me fine. I long to laugh at all the people I am and have been afraid of. She helps me to do this.

She is twenty-four and has just given birth to her fourth child in five years. Her marriage is almost finished, and both her mind and body are bruised black and blue. Her mad husband slinks about the house fondling his beloved cats. I rarely see him.

It is time to return to you, Mama. I tell you all about Con, but you are remote. No one has miseries comparable to yours. But why? He is in hospital now. We don't have to put up with His feebly whining presence any more. You have started teaching in various schools to earn our keep. You are exhausted permanently, and I am permanently guilty. But you never ask my help, or teach me to help. Life becomes so drab. I miss the excitement of being with Con. I remember how animatedly she talks, her vivid imagery and gestures. I will try it myself.

I have learned so much more than my contemporaries at school. And so I begin a year of lies. I can really flip their minds. At last I have some friends of my own, and can keep them successfully entertained. It is intoxicating, but I do get very mixed up at times. I can't keep track of all these imaginary events. It becomes terrifying in case I trip up. The other girls are sharp. I myself have sharpened them. They want more and more, and I cannot feed them. I begin not to know what is true and what I have made up. You know nothing of this Mama. I am quite alone within myself. He is going to die.

You ask me to visit Him in hospital. I have to make the journey alone, you explain how. I stand at the bus stop. I have forgotten the way. Buses come and go. I wait, the tears pouring down my face. I am so sorry, I have forgotten the way to Daddy. Finally I go back home. I tell you He is fine. You say He will die very soon now, and I must go to Con again.

This time her husband has gone. The house hums with activity, laughter, flirtation, fun. Con has filled it with lodgers to pay the bills. She is having an affair with a forcefully magnetic Arab, Izmet. I fall for him, instantly. But there are plenty of men to go round. I am constantly in love now. Very romantic. Clueless. I sit in the kitchen, listening to a conversation between two Turkish boys as to whether, in this country, fourteen is 'under age'. I realise it is me they are discussing, but I am neither frightened nor offended, only intrigued. Unaware of my own defencelessness.

We plan a party. Tart ourselves up, get everyone to help prepare food, music, decoration. The first guests arrive. The telegraph boy arrives. Daddy has died. She hands me the telegram in silence. I read it, and we both begin to laugh and laugh. Standing in the hallway, clutching each other, doubled up with hysterical laughter. We start to dance together, whirling round and round. We each grab a partner. Everyone is drawn into the dance, crazily gay. The room is bright and hot and noisy. I see her go out with Izmet. More guests come. A tall, usually grave Dutchman asks me to dance. I sober up to match his mood. He asks how my father is today and I tell him, offhandedly, just how dead Daddy is, breaking off to twirl under his arm and away. His shocked face, receding among the happy ones. I don't care. I have forgotten the way.

Father

I have forgotten
placed deep in the brittle centres
of my brain
the creep of spinal sweat,
threat of your voice in my ear
penetrating weird primal strains
from unknown vocal strings
far back in my throat.

I have forgotten
that you were not usually mad,
merely applying efficient principles
of time and motion
to me.

15

Memory is a syphilis
contracted when you screwed me
with electricity, and detachment.

I have even forgotten why
(obscenity of all)
you wanted to preserve me,
would not let me die
forgotten.

Dearest Mama,
Fifteen. Pages fluttering through my hands. I have ceased
living in the world. I have no friends. There was one,
when I first came to the new school. Elizabeth, brilliant,
lonely, fascinating to converse with, both of us badly
needing a friend. But at the end of the first term, standing
beside her in the classroom, listening to the marks being
read out, coming last in every subject, I catch sight of
her astonished, dismayed face. I have no explanation
for her. Thus it has always been for me. Up to now, we
rejoiced in each others company, happy in being 'different'
together. Now it emerges that we are also different from
each other. I don't expect it to change our relationship,
but it does. She is frightened off, and I take off with a
flock of books.

There is only one place to sit when the classrooms are
locked during the intervals. It is in the girls' washroom, a
noisy place but warm, where I perch on a wooden draining
board in the corner to escape into a book. And there, in the
eye of the storm of my life, I am safe, I am preserved. To
open a book is to enter a world of feeling, to be moved as
sweetly or as violently as the words permit, and to be able to
close the book, seal off the feelings, keep them safe between
the covers. Books are my drug.

David has come home. He limps, he has hurt himself. But the specialist can find nothing wrong, because he is the wrong specialist. David does not get better. I awake in the dark, to hear the sound of scrubbing. Going to his room, I find him with a look of terror on his face, scrubbing the carpet. He begs me not to stand on it, as it is unclean, will contaminate me. Another night, hearing running water, I leave my bed to find he has been washing his hands for hours. He holds them up, red, raw, trembling, to show me how everything he touches sticks disgustingly to them. I don't understand. Nobody understands. You, Mama, let him stay home, vaguely troubled by advice from the rest of the family to kick him out if he won't get a job, but not understanding that he is losing his mind, that he has been scared literally out of his wits.

David does not get better.

Walking to school. Walking back from school. Sitting in dusty classrooms, avoiding eye contact, I make myself a shadow. In the washroom with a book I am not a shadow. I am real, moving through a story. The girls around me are shadows, occasionally annoying me by interrupting. Any time not spent reading is interruption. So I stop going to school, appearing just often enough to prevent a serious inquiry. Cunning in my self-preservation, I perfect your handwriting, Mama, so that I can present notes of excuse for absence from you. I awake only enough to make time to dream the necessary dreams that provide practice in feeling with least risk.

Elizabeth, who has long since retreated in confusion, approaches me one day. She wants me to accompany her to a dance, our first. She is flustered in her innocence, does not trust the vaunted sophistication of the other girls, but wants to sample the delights of flirting in safety. I am flattered and excited, though sceptical of the attractions of mere boys. Yes, we will go together.

I stand at the bus stop next morning, flipping a mental coin as to whether to go to school or not. And suddenly, he is there, the fellow who took me home last night, embraced me under the dark trees, kissed my shadow face to life. He is not a boy, he is a young man, and he has come to me, unable to wait till our next date. This, then, must be love.

I remember standing at another bus stop not knowing the way, Mama. Is this the way? I sit on your bed, chattering eagerly to your gently smiling eyes. You are reliving the day you first met Daddy. You are not cautious for me, Mama. Just as you were not cautious for yourself at first. For the young man is not going to take me from this long, taut dream of a life I am living. In courting and marrying me, he, too, is going to enter it. We will live in the dream together, hardly noticing as the dream gradually turns nightmare. Only in the extreme pain of our son's reaction do we awake, groping fearfully in the dark for a light.

David

He travels time
ranges the wild and woolly west
(claims he has territory somewhere),
probes into outer space
and on the African savannas
shoots all the natives
as a chosen star-child's right.

Sometimes he comes upon a coastline,
follows it round awhile,
longing to meet himself and know
he's on an island
yet afraid.
He'd have to chart it, plant it, harvest it
and trade with other islanders
across the sea.

So he retreats inland
where space is limitless
and there is time to travel
a waste of time.

PART 2

Adult

Dearest Mama,

Something is wrong with Steven. He wears a look of constant anxiety and misery on his face — a child should not look like that. So I have been taking him to Child Guidance for tests. It is a large, old building that somehow manages to be warm and friendly too. Mostly I wait for Steven in a playroom with Frances. They said it would be all right to do that, and Frances loves it, of course. While I'm waiting, a woman comes in to 'take a history', as she puts it. She sits filling up boxes on a form. I'm in one of the boxes now, ready to be filed away. That's how I feel about my life at the moment. Each day is worse to face than the last. It is getting to the stage where, if I can just get through a day without one single attack of anxiety, it has been a good day. Even if it has felt as if I were wading in treacle, knee-deep in a quagmire of treacle, my perception of outside events is a sort of perpetual slow-motion. At least there have been no panic attacks lately. They are really horrible when they come, and quite uncontrollable.

Mama, where is she? She is so late today. There is this feeling slowly rising in me — the worst I can ever remember having. It is not panic. There is a lump in my throat, and my eyes are full of tears. It is strange, but I am beginning to think it has something to do with her not being here. Yes, that is what it is. And I remember when I felt it before. It is you, Mama, abandoning me again. Only now I cry woman's tears — for a woman I have hardly begun to know. Am I going crazy?

It is true that the last few times we were together, she didn't bother too much with the forms. Once, she pointed out how Frances always interrupted if I had to answer a difficult question, as if my little girl sensed my lack of ease and tried to help me. At home I have been uneasy for years, Mama. Anxious, prone to depression. Is Steven picking that up too?

I feel so safe with this woman, somehow. One time there was a very long silence when I didn't know an answer.

21

Normally I would have answered anything, even a lie, rather than endure such a silence. But with her it was very natural, easy, and in its own way, eloquent.

I have seen programmes on television where they show new techniques for communicating with brain-damaged 'hopeless cases'. It was profoundly moving to discover the hidden intelligence locked away for years, the sense of humour, the sudden shaft of hope. It is just like that with me, Mama. I am not brain-damaged, but I am nonetheless damaged. She sits with me, and it is as if, looking into my eyes, she is saying silently, 'I see you in there'.

I am in here, Mama. I had almost forgotten that I do exist, that I do matter. I have never allowed anyone in to really see me, in case, having seen me, they would turn away, as I have turned away from myself.

She is coming. I am happy, so Frances is happy. It is as simple as that, Mama. Happiness is blossoming in the playroom, alongside the terror of its loss.

The best gift she has given me so far is respect. When I ask her about the children, she amazes me by affirming that I am the expert there, not her. She asks me what I think, and I am astonished to find that I have not been doing too badly. She never makes the smallest decision for me, even when I invite her to, so that I am beginning to get the message. The choice is always mine. I have the resources within me to live my life, no matter what happens. No matter what has happened.

A dream. I steal a doll from the playroom, take it home under my coat. Later on, tidying the toys, I see that the doll is coming to life. I panic, thinking I have stolen someone's baby. But no, it does not belong to anyone else, it is mine, it is me. I am beginning to stir, beginning to let the feelings come through, beginning to come alive.

Psychotherapist

Electric lady
falling silent once again.

You lift the hair on my head,
voices stream out.

Circling the room they fly,
faster than fanned flames.

I catch them, cradle them,
crackling in my palms.

Charged with lit meaning,
lighting up memory.

Look what you've done,
my hands are burned.

And all that you can say
is 'yes, I know.'

I watch your scarred hands
winding the silence in.

And speak in altered tone
to answer you.

Dearest Mama,
I've been coming up this hill every week now for two
months. Leaving the main road, I cross at the lights and
enter the side street that leads to the hill, accompanied by
two of my children. As we walk, I explain to Steven how
this journey is so familiar to me I could do it blindfold.
I show him where my primary school is situated, quite near
the clinic we are now attending. The deadening private
school to which you sent me from the far side of the city,
because it was socially the best. I get so angry retracing my
small schoolgirl footsteps. For nine years I made that long
journey, alone and walking in dreams.

I suppose I have been angry with you for so long, about so many things, and so secretly, that I cannot bear to understand it all at once, Mama. Even from the first, this journey created a sense of impending danger. At the beginning I was barely conscious of this, for I liked going. It grew increasingly sweet to be cared for so intentionally and comprehensively by my therapist. Walking up the hill, I feel as if the pink petals of a rose in my breast are opening towards her. But I know that, as the final petal folds back, the black hairy spider crouched in the centre will at last be revealed to both of us. I am afraid, Mama. I am so afraid.

Steven has gone off for play therapy. Frances and I are in the playroom together, waiting, playing, waiting. It's all right this time. I saw her car as we came in. And suddenly she arrives, bearing my future. She leads me from the little playhouse chairs to the adult chairs where we will begin the work of my reconstruction.

It always begins with my children, how are they, what's been happening in the family this week, and so on. At first I answer objectively. But I love my children very much. When I speak of them, I reveal my love, my fears for them, and in doing so, I reveal my own fears. That is her cue to work with me. I give her the material, wrapped in my concern for the children. She unwraps it, to show me myself. I try to stop her doing this. I catch on very quickly to her technique. Each time I figure out afterwards just how she has managed to gently ease back another petal of the rose. It is no use. For each time she succeeds in a different way, a way I am not expecting.

I test her. I do not want to put my foot on a rotten branch. There is a tiny but wild hope beginning to stir in me, but I am very, very cautious. So often I have seen kindness turn cold when the one being helped is not sufficiently grateful and dependent. I must protect myself. I put up hoop after hoop for her and she jumps through them all, elegantly and with ease. She knows I am doing it before I do.

24

Thinking about the sessions at home, I can remember only a fraction of what is actually said. There comes a point where I have a clear memory only of her eyes. The room has faded away, the toys, Frances, time itself shifts from my consciousness. Her alert, intuitive eyes hold me. The warmth of her deep voice surrounds my clumsy answers, drawing out the thoughts within my stumbling words, the elusive feelings within my thoughts.

I am slowly coming to realise that I am disabled, Mama. I, who once moved about my life quickly, decisively, actively, looking as if I was in charge of it, am breaking down. I have been disabled all of my life. And my disability is just this: I do not know what I am feeling. Within me there is a defensive barrier that divides me from myself. I can pass through this barrier, be completely on one side of it or the other, but each state is mutually exclusive.

In other words, dearest Mama, I am just like you.

To the therapist, bringing a parent in to the waiting room of the Child Guidance Clinic.

You bring her in,
place her gently in a chair
to await her child.

She sits,
a red flower blooming in a chair,
red-tipped fingers
at rest on her lap.
It hasn't begun to dawn on her yet,
those things you said.

Carefully moving around
these broken people
in the warm wooden rooms
of this building.

As if you knew
how fragile flowers are
bearing their seeds.

Dearest Mama,

Today the appointment is at a different time. Some reason for this has been given, but it doesn't matter. I would come any time she asked me to. I sit in a hard upright chair four feet away from where she sits, also in a hard chair. We are alone in her room.

She lifts the phone and speaks into it, giving instructions not to be disturbed for an hour and a half. An immense relaxation seeps through me. I know she has done this intending me to hear.

She asks about Him. Where do I begin? I remember a certain beating I got once. I tell her this. I tell her of my confusion when, at the end, He suddenly picked me up and cuddled me.

I am a little child speaking, Mama, begging for reassurance, for some understanding that has never reached through to me.

She is talking now, her voice gentle. She explores with me what I must have learned from that. You always learn something. Chaos is intolerable, some kind of sense has to be made of it. Some kind of pattern has to be perceived, so that pain and shock are at least predictable.

She asks me what the very worst was. My mind descends into far distant silences. Eyelids almost closed, I shut her out. Slowly, without my volition, my hands spread in front of my face between us. I cannot. No, this is not going to be possible.

Her voice is so gentle now. She reminds me that we have one hour and a half. I can take my time. Again the huge wave of relaxation, something somewhere being released, flooding my being.

It is my voice speaking. The words come from me. I do not choose them. It is that little child inside me again. The little child who has been imprisoned for so long. Thirty years.

And now it is her voice, no longer gentle. Cool, crisp, undramatic. She hears the little child, she knows how upset it is, crying and crying. I have turned away from her, twisted right round in my chair so that she will not see my ugliness, my apology of an existence. But she is not speaking to the little child. She is addressing me, the woman.

'Have you heard of Child Sexual Abuse? Do you know what it means?' No, I haven't. I don't know. I am only little, only six. How should I know?

She is waiting for me to speak aloud and I can't. I hear her voice again. I want her to hold me so much, so tight, to hide my face against her, never to be alone again. But there is only the question — 'What does the term Child Sexual Abuse mean to you? What does it mean?'

Over and over again the words break through the trapped nightmare screams in her calm, confident voice. She is not horrified, not revolted. She is not even surprised. What does the term Child Sexual Abuse mean? It is taking me so long to remember, so long to emerge from the clamour the child is making. But the question is insistent, repeated and repeated, and the room slowly reconstitutes itself to my consciousness. I know where I am again, gradually realise that the done thing is to answer a question. I struggle for recall, embarrassed at so much hesitation. How could I be so stupid? What *is* Child Sexual Abuse? Why, it is ghastliness, it is horror, it is perversion. As an adult I know that, I can answer that. And the child, crouching, trembling within me, listens, understands, and is suddenly set free.

She nods at my answer. She has enabled me to calm my own anguish. It was not my fault. It was not my fault.

27

It was not my fault. I am exhausted, gasping, sweating with sheer relief.

Do you hear, Mama? I was innocent. I owe you nothing.

Friend

Harsh grief
spilling
into the sunlit stillness.

You stayed
listening
watching the strips of bandage
peeling off.

Blood
oozing on to a patch of sunlight
on the floor.

Years of loneliness
falling from tired eyelids.

Your stillness
embracing me.

'Feel it,'
your silence said.

'It really happened.'

Very still.
Years of afternoons
slid by.

Way back sometime.

Finally
a small, incredulous,
sunlit smile.

Dearest Mama,

I have been so involved with the image of myself as primarily your daughter all my life. That was my most important role. Not wife, not mother, not person in my own right. I hardly know who I really am at all, separate from you. I don't know what I actually want, need or expect from life. I only know what you expected me to want. What you expected for yourself and were disappointed in, you laid on me as a charge, and I took on your burden willingly, lovingly, protectively. What finally cracked me was my inability to do it for you, though I hardly knew what it was you wanted me to do. I only knew your subtle disapproval when I disobeyed your unspoken directives. You had such power over me, Mama, for one who was so apparently helpless.

And you, too were somebody's daughter. You used to quote her to me often, your mother. Combing out the tangles in my long hair every night, you would tell me how she said, 'You have to suffer to be beautiful.' I look into the dark determined eyes staring at me from a faded Edwardian photograph, and I ache for you, Mama. Nothing was ever good enough for her either.

You were the middle girl of three, daughters of a working-class family in a small town in Kent. Your face lights up when you speak of the sunny orchards where you only had to reach out to pick a ripe peach from the summer branches. I used to think it must have been like the garden of Eden, before the fall.

I don't know very much about your early childhood. I know you loved your father greatly, as did your sisters. I know he never talked down to you, and that this must have developed the huge intelligence that each girl needed to advance your mother's plans. I also know that you watched your mother's agitation and despair at his simple male pleasures, and his kindness to strangers in trouble. She despised him for that. Is that how you learned to revere and despise men simultaneously, Mama?

It was so long ago, another era. You moved in a stifling

climate for women. Long skirts of dark, serviceable stuff. Hard, hard work for low wages. The fear of illness, poverty, hell. The fear of sex. When you were thirteen, you won second place in a national music competition. Second top in the whole of England, Scotland, Ireland and Wales. Your heart was broken because you 'only' won the silver medal, not the gold. And you knew you should have won the gold, that you were really better than the winner. Did your mother understand? I don't know what she said, only that she was cross with you for skipping your music lesson for two weeks, because you were afraid to face your music teacher.

It is only with hindsight that I can fit all the pieces together. Your two sisters. Faith, who graduated with first class honours in history, and was the first woman ever to be offered a lectureship in that subject. Anne, who studied in America with the foremost pioneers in dietetics, at a time when the field was entirely new. And you, Mama.

They took you away from school. You only had an elementary education. I never knew it, till one evening a year ago when we both got a little tipsy. It was your most shameful secret. They just didn't have the money, you said. But they had the money for your music lessons. It was a choice they had to make. And because each daughter had to be a brilliant success, so that your mother could, in some convoluted way, better herself through them, it was music for you.

What does it mean, 'to better yourself', Mama? You used the phrase so often, with such certainty of being understood and agreed with. As your mother must have done. Both of you assuming with such utter pathetic conviction that you were not good enough as you were.

So you practised six, seven, eight hours a day, day after day, year after year, alone in a room with a keyboard throughout your adolescence. Every week you would take your music to be criticised by your music teacher. She gave you your faultless technique. She developed you socially too, made sure you understood etiquette, taught you how to be a lady. You carried out her huge demands unquestioningly. You owed it to your mother. You suffered to be beautiful.

And then finally, the last exam passed, the triumphs began. The first concert in the Queen's Hall, London. The second. The third. The fourth. You couldn't go on. You couldn't take the physical, emotional strain of the fear that accompanied each performance. No one had warned you about that. No one had prepared you for the churning stomach, the weak limbs, the sweating, slippery fingers, the sleepless nights preceding each occasion, the last desperate rehearsals.

There was no one to share the despair with, was there, Mama? No one could possibly know the lifetime invested in those four concerts. You never told me what your mother said when you gave up your career, but by then no words could possibly have reassured you. You were a disappointment to her, no matter what she said. Alone of your sisters you had failed. And you had no other education.

And then, He came, with His boyish charm, razor-sharp wit, enthusiasm for you and vast, all-embracing education. You worshipped Him. You saw His need for a lady-wife, which you filled perfectly. You both needed to better yourselves. Neither was good enough.

He came in the nick of time. You capped the academic achievements of your sisters after all. You married.

Images of you as a small girl, reaching for a peach in a warm orchard. Now you are older, reaching for success. Now you are a hurt woman reaching out, not for another human being, but for an idea, everyone's idea of a woman's ultimate success, marriage, motherhood, safety from failure. Your mother could not criticise. Your sisters were silent, disgusted, alienated. This time, you were the winner.

And so you plucked the peach from the branch and bit it. But you had no idea of the worm burrowed inside its flesh,

31

or how you would be forced to chew and swallow every last loathsome coil of it.

Pianist

Mother
foot-bound, mind-bound,
they couldn't bind your hands.

And when at the grand piano,
eyes, shoulders, arms, hands, keys
looped to a tight circle,
within which, disciplined
to a taut economy of effort,
you powered with ease the tenderness
of Schumann, I heard your protest,
yes, and I heard your moan,
lone woman.

Fluttering hands that never flew,
you let me know your burden,
you made sure I knew.

I also learned to play, have to unlearn.
I have to break the circle
have to return to words to say
what troubles me.

Dearest You,
You are not my mother any more. You are no one's mother.
You are cut loose, free at last to be just yourself.

It is three weeks since your death. You died in peace, and I am profoundly thankful for that, and for the fact that your last week was radiantly happy.

So we had a funeral to return your body to the earth. The service was beautiful, with flowers and friends and family, and all your favourite music. Everyone cried a little, and laughed a little when your small great grandson, peering into the grave, almost fell in.

Then we all said our goodbyes and departed into our own lives again. And though most of us have lived far away from you, we find that your absence creates a sudden, subtle shift in our lives.

At first I was continually being hurt by the fact that 'life goes on'. I would hear a concert on the radio that you would have enjoyed, or see the Japanese cherry tree flowering, and remember that I will never share that with you again. Once, I found a pack of old photos, and thoughtlessly opened them. There you were, deep in earnest discussion with my son, and there I was, sitting on the bed with the photo in my hand, whimpering and sobbing as if a newly stitched wound had suddenly been torn open. After that, I knew quite objectively that I had loved you intensely. And I also knew that my immense doubt on the subject had been caused by the conflict within me between that intense love and an equally ancient anger.

You never protected me against Him. I know now why this was. I think you lived much of your life in a state of continual depression. As a result you were blind and deaf emotionally to most of what went on around you. Your stance was one of defence against the possible attack, criticism or slight to which you were so vulnerable. But your defences safeguarded you from the reality, particularly when reality was threatening. Married to Him, how could reality be other than threatening?

You failed to protect me against Him, not only in the physical sense, but in the very core of my being. You laid me open and defenceless by your constant championing of Him. You lied to yourself and to all around you for self-protection, so that you would not confront consciously the loneliness of responsibility that, in the end, you had to cope with anyway. In doing so, you forced me to live with two versions of Him – your version, and the one I actually experienced. Somehow I managed to contain these extremely polarised images of Him and accept them both as true. For me it was crucial that at least one of you must be trustworthy, so I could not risk facing the implications of challenging your word. Such a juxtaposition of inconsistencies was possible only at great cost to my own appreciation of reality. But I learned, from you, how to achieve it.

Your deep fear and disapproval of sex was as present in that bedroom with Daddy and me as if you had been there yourself. Your disapproval *was* you, to such an extent that as a child I thought you must know. Your rejection of me was a logical result. My guilt for what I thought I had done to you sat toadlike in the back of my mind, for in a thousand ways you said, 'Daddy is always right'. Most clearly of all when you let your own daughter be excluded from the family. I took the warning. In silence, I accepted the guilt, not Him. It was the explanation for anything I suffered after that. I knew I deserved no better. My life was spent trying to make it up to you, to please you by becoming the success you wanted me to be, and failing. Yet I wanted to fail. I did not deserve to succeed. And so I could never appease your disapproval.

And that is why the anger and the love are going to be my constant companions from now on, whenever I think of you as my mother. The one does not cancel out the other. They both exist, jagging sharply into each other, so that I can never think of you peacefully. Except when I see you not as my mother, who let me down, but as you, in all your humanness, another woman like myself, with failures and greatnesses, and a deep and lonely struggle to contend with.

Way Out

And so I fold sheets,
iron, join old shreds of cloth
to make new sheets,
wash them, make beds,
wait for the way out of this one.

Before
it was so easy,
I simply went to sleep, my shawl
a book, TV, a church, a crowded street,
subtracted self from fear
till all was over, but the weeping.

For years I hid in that dead-silent shroud,
then spoke aloud
and woke myself in mid-sleepwalk.
I nearly broke the thread.

But found the other way,
that leap in distance, trusting to be caught
which brought myself to bear
a new child
me.

Now, to simply be,
with no wild searching, weeping,
I sew my love a sheet, and wait,
unsleeping.

Dearest You,
Yesterday I went to visit Catriona. We are going to read
some of these letters and poems to a group of women who
have suffered incest and sexual abuse. There are so many
of us.

I had never met Catriona before. We hit it off immediately, then spent several hours just getting to know each
other. She is younger than me, small, curly-haired, pretty,
vivacious. We went to her flat to rehearse, and then I found,
all over again, how difficult it is for me to relive these events
person-to-person. It was very harrowing, and at times I had
to stop and deep-breathe quietly for a few minutes before

I could continue. Then something quite remarkable happened. Quite unlooked for.

We came to the part where Daddy dies. 'She hands me the telegram in silence. I read it and we both begin to laugh and laugh.' Much to my consternation, Catriona started to laugh. Right out loud. I was a bit disconcerted for a minute because I thought, 'That's not what your're supposed to do. This is tragic.' And I tried to keep reading, but I just couldn't, because I found that from some terribly deep part of me, I was laughing too.

I will never forget the sight of that small figure rolling about in a big armchair, holding herself, tears of laughter streaming down her cheeks, gasping, 'Thank God he's dead! Thank God he's dead!' And I too, could not stop the deep chuckles of laughter bubbling up from my gut. It seemed to go on and on, and I just let it. I don't think I have ever in all my life been so helpless to control my laughter. It was not hysterical laughter this time. It was good, big, deep belly laughter. Every time I thought it was coming to an end it seemed to renew itself and gather, and erupt again, and then we'd look at each other laughing and just let it all happen. And so, together with this suddenly dear, close stranger, in the space of a few minutes, I finally buried Daddy for all time.

Today my insides feel too big for my rib cage. It seems to have done something to my anatomy. Stretched out whatever tight places were left. Undone the last knots. I phoned Catriona, and she said she felt the same way. She had needed it almost as much as me — and it hadn't even happened to her.

Over the last few months I've been able to feel more and more. It has been like learning to use an invisible, atrophied limb whose existence was previously unsuspected. I've felt mostly grief and anger. It has been sharply and almost constantly painful, coming alive. And yet, throughout everything, I've known that this 'knowing what I'm feeling' is health, is normality. I've realised for some time the importance of crying, the value of shared tears. But I could never have estimated the value of shared laughter. Everything is becoming more and more real.

A Photo of Me

Snap!
And suddenly
I see my total beauty
trapped in a photograph.
The whole of my taut dream
caught in the still laughter —
or could it be a scream
at seeing death approach
that nick of time?
I only know
that I have clicked with me,
and nothing after
quickens with quite the same life's breath.

Dearest You,
I was walking with my small daughter, her hand in mine, through a late spring this morning. High overhead, vapour trails criss-crossed where planes had flown earlier through the blue translucence, and now they hovered motionless, speaking of journeys taken at speed over our heads as we had slept. It was hot, though still quite early. The road we walked along was flanked with trees and bushes heavy with blossom, hawthorn, horse chestnut, rhodedendron, like gigantic bouquets offering themselves to us as we passed. Now and then, a shower of golden laburnum shimmered in the morning heat, poised, ballerina-like, dancing without moving, as a joyful soul does.

It is a pleasant area we live in, quite near the house where I was born. I remember when we bought this house, and I knew you would approve of it, so I approved of it. Later, when we thought of moving, I lay awake at night feeling lost at the thought of living far away somewhere. As if I knew I had to find myself here, first, before taking the risk of being lost forever.

The houses are large, each surrounded by its own beautifully arranged garden with well-maintained fences, hedges and walls between neighbours. In spring and summer nature is lavish, spilling out into the quiet roads from the gardens, filling the air with colour and scent. I love to walk these streets with my little girl, who is full of wonder and curiosity about everything. I point out each tree and flower by name, we talk about the families who live in the houses, grand stone residences, as mine was. There is one house with a coloured climbing frame in the garden. It is the childrens' residential home. But they are very quiet, although there are twenty children in care. They are not to be seen much, the tall walls contain them so that you would hardly know they are there. But they are there.

I used to haunt the area surrounding my school on the other side of the city like this. The other day, passing some familiar gates in the car, I stopped on impulse, got out of the car and gazed long and hard at the gates. There was a notice, 'No entrance except on business'. I entered.

I walked through that school from one end to the other, from the ground floor to the top floor and back down, filled with a kind of ecstasy, saying hello and goodbye to each landmark recognised, joy and relief alternating with the memories of fear, sadness and loneliness evoked at every turn, now able to tell myself, 'Yes, that happened, but it's over. Everything is going to be all right.'

For me, Mama. But what about all the others?

When I returned to the ground floor and went along the main corridor, in the centre of which is the foyer where the head teacher's room is, I saw it was blocked off by a barrier of chairs spread from wall to wall with the sign 'No Passage' on one of them. And there in the middle of the foyer she stood, imposing and dignified in her black academic gown, observing my approach with an expression I was not able to fathom. She did not know who I was, and yet I was obviously familiar and at ease. I knew my way about, and I was not going to be turned back by a line of chairs and a sign.

As I was about to pass her, she stopped me. Refusing politely her offer of help, I was about to proceed when she asked me, a little more forcefully, what my business was in the school.

I stopped. And as I turned to answer her, it suddenly struck me that this woman was in a position to help, or set on the road to help, all those many hurt children who pass through her school unnoticed, as I did so many years ago, unnoticed by her predecessor. I smiled at her. I asked her if she could spare five minutes to talk. I explained that I had come back to look again with adult eyes at the school I had experienced so much unhappiness in. She blinked nervously, backing away to her open doorway, saying that she was waiting for a telephone call, had only wished to know who it was who was walking through her school.

And so I left, walking swiftly and cheerfully away down the corridor, out of the side door and into the brilliant sunshine. It was only as I was fitting the key into my car door that I felt the tears come, tears of sadness and frustration at my inability to unlock that heart, unlock all the hearts who do not know, cannot see who it is who walk our schools, walk our streets, walk the terrifying rooms of their memories, of their dreams, of their trapped lives.

And yet I cannot blame her. I think back to my three years in a college of education, where I specialised in psychology. They taught me how and why rats and pigeons learn to press bars, but not how to recognise a hurt child, or even that hurt children exist. In their nice, safe, academic world hurt children do not exist. But in the classroom, struggling with my task as a young teacher, I found out how many of them do. At least three or four in every class, unable to learn because of the turmoil of their emotions, the energy needed to learn given instead to learning to survive. In the effort to hide the truth from outsiders, to cope alone, all things childish, play, curiosity, fun, wonder, have to take second place, have to be discarded completely if necessary.

Whose fault is it, Mama? I have blamed myself, I have blamed you, I have blamed my father, I have blamed my teachers for not being more perceptive, society for not wanting to know. Can anything change, Mama? I speak to your spirit that knows everything now, can accept the truth at last. I speak to the spirit of my first adult friend, Margot, who suffered incest and whose body refused to grow into a woman's, so that at twenty-five she still had the body of a fear-filled twelve year old, frozen into the moment of her father's assault. I think of that small body now, laid in the earth, destroyed by its own hand. Can anything change?

Maybe the first thing that has to change is all this blaming.

Staffroom

Habitually
they progress
stitch by stitch,
work through the printed pattern
of a garment for their warmth
and harmlessness.

Small talk unwinds a ball of thought
and finds its way in,
over, through and out
they know not what,
except that it is dangerous,
is doubt.

Their fear
stares at me, paused in the door,
unsure,
causing a draught.

Dear Dad,
As I start to write this letter, I also start to weep. I look at
those first two words — 'Dear' and 'Dad', and it seems to me
that I have never in my life put two words together that
were more incongruous. I keep looking back at them
incredulously as I write, to see if maybe the conventional
way of starting a letter will somehow, by its sheer electric
shock value, cut through the block of stone that encases the
thought of you within me.

The most positive emotion I can feel for you is pity. I
want to forgive you, not for your sake. My forgiveness can
mean nothing to you now. I want to forgive you because I
have survived you for so long, and now I am finding more
each day that surviving is not living. And I want to live. Do
you know what that means, or were you, too, a survivor?

'Forgive and forget' is the saying. I forgot you. For years
I didn't dare remember you consciously. I buried you alive
in my brain, but your image was reflected in the eyes of
every man who looked at me. Every man who wanted me
was you. You lay in my bed each night. In my fantasies, in
my dreams you were there, always in disguise, but the terror
was the same terror and it was real. Not daring to recognise
you, I didn't know where it was coming from, so I couldn't
face it. Had I faced it alone, I would have lost my mind.
So I waited until I had help.

I met and married a man of goodwill. As unlike you as I
could find. And when I found him, I clung on to him,
burdening him, dragging him down with the heavy weight
of my fear, my anger and resentment at you, at Mama.
Gradually he lost his sparkle, his enthusiasm, his joy in life,
and assumed a permanent mantle of anxiety and care for

me, your victim. So we became not husband and wife, but rescuer and victim, just like you and Mama, though we played the game less viciously.

It gives me no pleasure to know that you would be proud of your three grandchildren. They do possess all the traits you valued, and many qualities you did not know how to value. But their chief value to you would be that they were 'your' grandchildren. You would look into their eyes, as you did your own children, searching to see if they had what it takes to be worthy of being in 'your' family. You had no idea of the intrinsic worth of each individual. You rejected so many people as not being up to par, that you created the illusion that everyone else was not quite the same superior species. And in that isolation, your cruelty reigned unchallenged.

You have hurt us all so much. Your cruelty reached right down to my children. You hurt them through me. My struggle was so difficult that I gave up finally. My despair, and the state of constant tension you left me in, affected them. How am I ever going to forgive you? How am I going to change pity into compassion?

I approach you as Perseus did the monster, blindfold, holding up the mirrored shield to you. But you are dead. If I keep reminding myself of that, I can take off the blindfold. I can really look at you.

In the folklore handed down to me about your past, your father is an indistinct presence. Your mother emerges, long red hair, beautiful, vicious in temper. Your sister surfaces, briefly and mysteriously. It was years before I even knew of her existence, and was immediately silenced on wanting to know more. I still know practically nothing about her, except that she died alone and painfully. I record her name because I want it to live, not be forgotten. Her name was Beth.

You were the second child of your mother, her pride and joy because you were legitimate, whereas Beth wasn't. She never forgave Beth for existing to remind her of her 'fornication'. Because Beth existed, she had to marry your quiet, gentle father, who was not Beth's father. In those times she could not refuse such an offer. She was lucky to get it. She knew that fact and raged against it, and against the living need for it, Beth, for the rest of her life. Her rage poisoned her marriage, her children, her grandchildren, her great-grandchildren.

Let me get behind your little boy's eyes, so that I can see too. I need to see so much. You saw her rages. She was a frightening woman. There was something about her sexuality that was rampant, but denied, inadmissible. There was something shameful about your sister, and it had to do with your mother's secret, which was a sexual one. You strained your sharp child's intelligence to work it all out, but she frightened you. She knocked your calculations askew.

From some small beginning, the seeds of your own violence began to grow. Perhaps she turned on you one day. Perhaps she played with your emotions, favoured your sister on a whim. Your sister was so starved for love. She was the household drudge, the 'skivvy'. You were given everything your small heart could desire. But you couldn't earn it, predict it, control it. You were helpless in the hands of this raging disappointed woman, and you feared and loved her with your whole, impotent child's strength.

What did you learn about women out of such confusion? Did you learn from your mother of their beauty, of their terror, of their sexual frailty? Did you learn from your sister that they could be cowed, tamed, verbally or physically bludgeoned into submission? Was it from your mother's lapse, from the living stigma that your sister was, that you learned of the shame that could come from the expression of female sexuality? Did you think that only disaster would come from allowing that expression?

Maybe that's why you chose safety, you chose Mama. Somehow you knew she agreed with you about the danger, perhaps by the very fact of your mutual silence on the subject. You kept her permanently pregnant, which ensured

43

her dependence on you, and her continual fear of discovering and delighting in her own sexuality. As compensation you named her and gave her all the trappings of a lady. But it wasn't enough for either of you.

I have your love-letter to her, written in my fifth year. It is the letter of a swain to his lady, of a little boy to his adored mother. It made me so angry when I saw it. That was the year you sent my sister away, because you couldn't bully her into giving up her fiancé. She was as strong-willed as you, and you couldn't have that. So you made of her a dreadful example, a warning to the rest of us.

What did you do with your own sexual feelings? Those frighteningly strong urges that you didn't dare share with Mama?

You were scared, gut-scared of whores. Your friends' wives were all ladies, and in any case your fear of a scandal was too great to risk an affair. Once, just once, you broke out of the dilemma with one of the maids, but you got caught. You nearly lost Mama. You had to be very clever about that. You were also cruel and callous. 'The best method of defence is attack' was your favourite chess rule. You believed it through and through.

Did you think I wouldn't understand? Did you imagine I was too small to feel? To feel fear, to feel turned on, simultaneously? Did you think, could you possibly imagine you could creep up on me, use me, without my knowledge? Were you so unaware that my living, sentient, shivering flesh would remember forever what my brain would refuse to recall completely and clearly?

It is the only way I can understand you. I was just your possession, like all the others. A part of 'your' family, the smallest, least important part, not a person at all, really. You didn't know the harm you were doing to me, nor did you care. You had the right to use your possession. I understand you, but I will never excuse you, Dad. You were the adult in the situation. You chose to refuse to grow up, but you *were* grown up. You had the ability to choose, and you chose to abuse that tremendous power you had over me, and to break my life.

Well you didn't succeed. I am pretty strong-willed too. I have slipped out of your influence, slipped out of the grasp of 'your' family. I have my own family now. We have been hurt, and in our pain we have lashed out at each other. But that is being healed.

I look back across the years at you and Mama. I see you as scared drowning children, clinging to each other, pulling each other underwater into a soundless colourless twilight world of loneliness. To see you as children, defenceless like I was, has helped me. I need to identify with you, because I want to understand, to feel compassion. But I can't feel compassion for you yet. There is this huge black gap I have to cross between your childhood and your fatherhood. At some point in that gap you decided against becoming all that you were capable of becoming. To excuse you because of your childhood would be to deny your human potential, as you denied mine.

I look back across the years and it seems that the recurring theme in all the long line of unhappy people is the inability to forgive. There is no middle way. It is either forgiveness or revenge. But rarely is it possible to take direct revenge. It gets twisted, distorted, disguised, put on to the wrong people, causing new ripples of pain to spread.

But I've found there is mercy in the world, there is forgiveness. There are people who have made different choices. I want to be one of them. I want to be the first in a long line of happy people. I believe that I was intended for happiness. And so I am still trying to find the lost way to you, because my instinct is that only through you can I achieve that quality of living I have seen in the eyes of others who have found the way to forgive.

I look back to the day I first spoke of what you did to me. I remember how the false guilt just fell away from me, like a heavy silk quilt slips from the body of a sleeper who suddenly turns. It did not leave me innocent. No adult can be

45

innocent. But it left me able to distinguish false guilt from real guilt. I saw my strengths. I also saw clearly, separate from any thought of you, my weaknesses, my many failures that have nothing to do with you. And I feel, dimly, very dimly, that it is this awareness of my own weakness that is perhaps going to free me to forgive you one day.

And now I want to stop looking back. I want to look forward instead. I don't know what I am looking forward to. That's the beauty of it. I'm going to find out.

PART 3

Family

Housebound

In a house
with a cellar
wine laid up
and a well in the cellar

some live in the attic
think
and think to see
everything

some run up and down stairs
between floors
sleep on the landings
walk upon carpets
shift sofas
paper their walls
and change the paper
seasonally

some live in the hall
keep an eye on the front door
lest any stranger
enter

install a peephole
peep.

Survivors. The word conjures up victims of an accident who
have somehow managed, against great odds, to live. Or
released victims of wartime concentration camps. People
who are alive, but only just by the skin of their teeth.

And when I read about those camps, survivors' accounts
of what they were like, I realise with a shock that, on some
level that is not physical, I have been there. I know about
being there. I know about the hunger and the cold. I know
about the tall barbed-wire fences, the searchlights, the dogs,

the importance of knowing one's correct position at roll-call, the importance of remembering one's number. My number was seven. I know about the day-to-day uncertainty, the searching for pattern, for meaning. I know about the self-effacement, the secret fantasies of what it would be like not to be small, trivial, powerless, hungry for love. I know how vital, but how dangerous these fantasies were.

I know about trying to hide tiny treasures in dark places, so that they can't be taken away. I know about trying to hide myself in a crowded classroom, in a crowded family, so that I won't be seen and brought forward for interrogation, ridicule, punishment, disgrace. And most of all I know about the guilt of it, that strange phenomenon by which the survivors come to accept the situation as normal, to forget any other way of life, to be so ashamed of being human in this animal squalor, that they pretend even to themselves that they are being correctly treated, because they *are* animals, disobedient, untrustworthy animals. The prisoners who are most obedient get a small reward, a position of special responsibility, a little extra food. Their hunger for love is falsely fed by a little praise, and they seem to get on well, but they are only successful prisoners. The others look on with envy, strive to be more obedient, seek for ways to please their captors, or ways not to be noticed, or ways to escape. There is no way to escape, except inwards, as my brother David did.

The family, grown up, attempt escape geographically, scatter, escape into forgetfulness, illusion, and the striving needed to try to turn that illusion of escape into reality. Each family member inhabits a separate world. Not only do they not want to remember, they cannot remember how it really was. Each is equally conscious of being the misfit in the family, and determines to make good nonetheless. The dread of never being good enough is constant. They carry around fences within fences for the rest of their lives. The inner fences, the most jagged wires of all, seal off the clear memory of the pain and humiliation. That is why every member of that family, sexually abused or not, is to some degree a survivor, a survivor of the accident of being born to parents incapable of seeing more than their childrens' material need, and sometimes not even that. Parents incapable of seeing themselves as guardians of their children while they grow, incapable of admitting this to themselves, to each other, or to any outsider.

But we who are the victims of sexual abuse live in a special cage, right in the centre of all the barbed-wire fences. It is the only place left to us of safety, the only place where our identity is preserved, the 'I' that is at the core of every being, male or female.

Recently I watched a film made at the end of the war, where people who had lived in the countryside surrounding a concentration camp were made to visit the camp, now liberated. Their faces, as they filed along the road, were smiling and carefree. It was a day's jaunt to them, some were carrying picnic baskets. They clearly had no idea of what they had been living so close to for years, or of what they were so soon to witness.

It was like that with my family. Nobody had the slightest idea of how things really were. We were under orders to be a large, jolly, rambling family, interesting, fun to be with, bound for great things. And so we were. We were so good at it that we completely fooled everyone. That we were equally successful most of the time in fooling ourselves and each other, was essential for our individual and family survival.

When I read about concentration camps, I am drawn again and again to speculate on what made men and women able to live comfortably in the midst of such devastation without seeming to have any feeling for the suffering they were inflicting, or allowing to be inflicted, upon fellow human beings. The answer of course is, that it was only possible for them because they did not see the prisoners as fellow human beings. On their arrival at camp, prisoners were put

51

through a systematic process of dehumanisation, at the end of which they knew that if they were allowed to exist at all, it was only for the purposes of their captors, and they were expected to be clean, compliant working machines. The repeated traumas that made up this process made them conform, for the most part, to this image of themselves, as a condition of existence.

Understanding how these survivors were terrorised and dehumanised helps to answer the question that is often asked about those other survivors, incest victims. 'Why do they put up with it in silence for so long? Why do they not tell some outsider?' And often, behind this question, there is a hidden accusation, an added burden to adult survivors, we who already accuse, judge and condemn ourselves for so much, forgetting the physical and psychological powerlessness of our position as children in abusive families. In those who ask this question accusingly, there is a certain lack of memory and imagination, the memory of their own smallness in relation to the adults around them and the imagination of the virtual impossibility of pitting that smallness against the total sum of adult power, even should they be quite clear that what was happening to them was legitimate cause for complaint.

Many of us are not that clear. To the child growing up in an ordinarily loving family, much happens which is not to her liking, which is imposed by adults in the normal course of discipline. It is not automatically clear to an abused or sexually abused child when parents have gone over the score, when we are being treated in a manner that is wrong. Many of us are specifically told that what is happening is usual, though private. As children we trust our parents. Or if from bitter experience we learn not to, neither are we disposed to trust anyone else.

Some of us are only too clear that what is happening to us is wrong. The reason we do not tell is simply that we are afraid of the violence we regularly observe or experience. We fear, or are told, that it will culminate in our death.

Given that we have been brought close to death, that we have lived in continual terror, that we may have seen brothers, sisters and mother slammed about the house unmercifully, may have suffered so ourselves, the threat of our own death is no idle threat. After all, no-one rescues the other members of the family, so why should we be safe?

Anyone who has been involved in a car crash knows the helplessness of being in a powerful machine moving at speed towards disaster, the sudden fragility of human bones as one is hurled through space against sharp corners, thrown at walls and road surfaces, cast into deep shock. A child in a violent household can live in permanent crash. There is no higher authority than father. Police seem reluctant to interfere, or may be an added source of threat rather than aid. To live in such a household is like travelling in a car being driven by an insane driver. We are cut off from any passing help. We know that if we cry out from the window he will simply speed up and kill us. He has told us so, and everything we know about him, about the world we live in, confirms it. Mother seems as helpless as we are, so there is no point in telling her. The line between physical and sexual abuse is a thin one to a child. She knows about the physical abuse, perhaps suffers it too, so perhaps the sexual abuse is just an extension of this.

Some of us have told our mothers, and still receive no help or response from her. This is very hard for us to understand, and makes it almost impossible for us to try again with an outsider. Our mother is so much bigger than us, so much wiser. It is inconceivable that she may see herself as a badly frightened child, perhaps also a survivor of incest, neglect or other abuse. Our telling her is akin to telling a bigger sister who is also bullied and oppressed by father. She may be in a position to listen and protect us, but equally, she may not. The results of her own childhood, together with the consequent conditions of her adulthood may have damaged her so much that she cannot connect

53

what she sees and hears to her understanding or imagination because it is simply too painful.

I think back to the years of depression and anxiety when as a mother, weighed down with my past, more lonely than I understood, running nowhere like a caged rat on its little drum, I missed seeing for so long the distress of my child. The effort of denial, the sheer fatigue of keeping everything normal-seeming when it wasn't, out of shame and fear of the stigma of not being a good mother, made me as blind and deaf as my own mother. But as well as not having her problem of sexual abuse to recognise, acknowledge and cope with, I was a thousand times more fortunate than her. My husband was not abusive. Hers was. My husband was open to the possibility that we needed help. Hers was arrogantly dogmatic that he and his family were perfect. I had somewhere to go for help, help that would be confidential, comprehensive, competent and free. Except on a superficial level, she was isolated, and knew nowhere to turn. Had my marriage broken up, I could have supported my children, with great difficulty. At the time my mother had no means of support at all, and had seven children. The break up of a home is always an agonisingly public affair, no matter how common it is, or what the social climate. But to break up a home which has been sexually abusive is to invite and receive more judgemental criticism than is able to be contemplated by a depressed, self-accusatory, friendless woman. Society not only condemns the abuser, but the mother. She is called collusive because she has not been able, for any of these reasons and many more, to put a stop to the abuse. She is called 'frigid', sexually unobliging to her husband, and she is blamed as much or even more than him, as though it were possible to achieve sexual intimacy with a man capable of incest, or, for that matter, any kind of intimacy. Like many women of her generation and up-bringing, my mother feared sex. But I have no doubt that, whatever went on in their bedroom, she had cause to fear it. As a child, young girl, young adult, client in therapy, I had not the objectivity to see this as I do now. But only those of us who have suffered have the right to anger, to allocate blame, for the sake of our own healing. Others merely increase the agony by failing to try to understand.

What tortures many of us is just this question — did my mother know? Even years later the uncertainty of how to approach, to feel about our mother, the barrier that has built up between our mothers and ourselves, the longing to talk about it with her, the fear of what might emerge if such openness were possible, all this is a crippling weight for us to carry. If we speak to her about it and find she has known then we have to readjust all our perceptions and find a way of living with them. If she has not known, and we tell her, she may reject and accuse us, or she may at last take us in her arms and give us the care we have wanted and needed for so long. This would be the most fabulous dream come true, a bubble we don't want to take the risk of bursting. I was lucky being able to release the tension of taking that risk. I had the chance of rehearsing that openness with a woman I had come to care for, to look to, just as if she had been my mother. Because I did care for her so much the risk was as real, but for me it paid off, not because I was able to find out if my mother had known, but because I was believed and accepted.

I can remember sitting with my brother David in the garden, wanting to tell him that my father was touching me in a way I hated. David was the most likely to sympathise, for he was in constant trouble, often harshly beaten, though by no means a naughty child. The very sight of him seemed to enrage my father. I can remember the long silence between us as I searched for the right words, the words a child doesn't have, to express the nausea, the disgust, the shame. In the end I couldn't do it. Extraordinary as it may seem, we were both so imbued with family propaganda that it seemed traitorous to even think, much less talk, rebelliously. Neither of us could mention misery. We were not supposed to be miserable.

My father did not threaten me overtly, as far as I can remember. But it is difficult to exaggerate the charismatic power of his personality. Confirmed by my mother's sweet submission, it was irresistible. Her gentility made it impossible for me to tell her, ever. I was too ashamed, too embarrassed to say the words. I knew they were not nice, that I was not nice either. To tell anyone at all was to betray my father, my mother, to explode the family success story, and to destroy myself in the process. For he did not need to beat me as he did David. The remotest threat of that possibility, together with its very occasional execution, was enough to make me let him do as he pleased. I let him, I allowed it, therefore it was my sin, and I deserved punishment.

And I think of the healing of the man born blind. It was not his blindness alone that was healed by Jesus. It was the fact that he had been led to believe himself a sinner from birth, and that this was the cause of his blindness. And I believe that it was the lifting of this heavy psychological burden, by gentle understanding and reassurance, that he was enabled to see. To see that he never had brought this affliction on himself, that he was the innocent survivor of an accident of birth.

I am drawn back again to speculate upon what made men and women able to look with equanimity on the devastation they caused. To commit terrible crimes against humanity, then go into the part of the the camp reserved for the camp commandants and eat a good meal with wine, chat with their wives, read a book or listen to the radio, ignoring the smell and the cries which must have penetrated those quiet comfortable rooms. It is an impossible feat, no one could believe it possible, or would, if we had not the evidence that it did happen, and is now a part of history.

Perhaps a clue to this enigma can be found in the realisation that the barbed-wire fences surrounded also the commandants' compound. The captors were also captive.

Unlike the prisoners, it was possible for them to take short breaks outside the camp, but they knew that they always had to come back. Their main task was to carry on extracting the last ounce of usefulness from the prisoners before disposing of them as efficiently as possible. They were under strict orders to do this. To do it willingly, even with relish, was perhaps the only way they had to survive the inner knowledge of the horrific things they did.

And so they stifled their conscience by studying and applying rigorously the laws of the regime which gave them status. This was the justification of all they did. And yet, it was well known among the prisoners that the most dangerous action one could take was to meet the eyes of one of the tormentors with a level gaze. To do this was to force him to acknowledge, even if only for one split second, that he was torturing a human soul like himself. To do this would be seen as an attack, would threaten his survival. For no-one could survive knowing the totality of another person's agony, together with one's responsibility in causing it. There is no law that will justify the infliction of suffering if the recognition of our common humanity is allowed to be glimpsed for a moment. And that is why the laws are vital to the survival of the captors. They always have to have a superior authority they can appeal to, to blind them to the pleading in their prisoners' eyes. But it is that same regime that keeps them imprisoned with the prisoners, that chains them to the dreadful round, the vicious circle which they, as much as the prisoners, are powerless to break out of without the help of an objective perception.

My father and mother were under orders. Their primary order was to succeed, at whatever cost, and to be seen to be successful. No mistake was tolerated by the regime, and so the slightest mistake had to be carefully covered up. Their children, being part of them, had to be part of the success story too, and had to learn and obey the regime. There were other laws also, equally rigid and unyielding. For instance

57

the prohibitive laws about sex, the duty above all else of obedience from wife and children, the crucial importance of a united family front of cheerfulness, togetherness and, most of all, success. My mother's first rule about wifely loyalty led her to completely overlook the fact that though she worshipped him, she didn't actually love my father. She didn't know this because she had never herself experienced any warm love. His death brought great relief to her, which fact in its turn brought shame.

Who was giving these orders to my parents? Who was this superior authority that they relied upon so much? In the first instance, they had started receiving orders about being, feeling, knowing and doing as infants, as toddlers, as children growing up, as adolescents, and as young adults. The orders were etched in their brain traumatically. So it seemed a naturally logical thing to continue receiving the echo of the orders about how to be, how to feel, what to know, what to do, to carry them into their parenthood, just as their parents had done. This was familiar in both senses of the word. This was unquestionably safe. And as long as there were no questions, no attempt at revolt among the prisoners, everything ran smoothly. But it is the nature of adolescents to question, and if no satisfactory answers are forthcoming, to revolt.

My father put down any attempt at revolt with savage repression. But the mere fact that his orders — *the* orders — had been questioned, shook him. Forced him, in the utmost secrecy of his heart, to question the necessity of his own imprisonment. Especially his sexual imprisonment. And somehow I stumbled in on this period of his heart's confusion, and he used me as an experiment to find out, in the safety of my uncomprehending silence, what it was in the way of sexual fulfilment he had been missing. He could not find out from me, for an adult can only find sexual fulfilment within a relationship freely chosen by another adult. But he didn't know this, for he had never experienced a truly free choice. All his life he had been under orders.

What does the inability to feel compassion do to the self? What does it do to lose the possibility of that dawning recognition of fellow-feeling in another person's situation, in another person's eyes? It is a disaster for the prisoners, at the mercy of laws and their cold logic. But no less is it a disaster for the captors. Not to know what it is like to feel compassion puts each individual captor in a state of utmost loneliness. For if they cannot imagine compassion, it is beyond their imagination that anyone could ever feel compassion for them. They can never be forgiven, nor forgive themselves for their weakness, their vulnerability, their many mistakes made in the attempts to carry out the impossible orders. They live in the same prison of untouchable shame that they have built with impregnable defences for their prisoners, their growing children.

The proportion of camp survivors to those who did not survive was not high. At first, it must have been difficult for the liberators to take in just what had been going on, not only the depth of the horror, but its massive scale. Ashes do not take up much room. But there were many unburied bodies, and each had to be checked for any remaining life, for many survivors looked dead, so emaciated and weakened had they become. And as the living looked like the dead, so did survivors resemble each other in their ragged uniforms. Only the gaunt eyes were expressive of the human soul, and sometimes even these windows were blank, for the survivor had escaped into insanity. Their gender could not be told by outer aspect, because that most obvious and innocent indicator, hair, had been shaved, so that men and women had the same appearance. The menstrual cycle of women was halted, sometimes permanently, by starvation and deprivation, so that not only in appearance, but in physical fact, they were de-feminised.

When the allied forces liberated the camps at the end of the war, the problems of dealing with the survivors must have seemed immense beyond imagining. The best they could do was to provide food, water, immediate medical care, clothing, blankets, transport back to the countries of origin. The survivors arrived home again, albeit to discover sometimes no home and no family. But they were alive, physically alive, with renewed strength and renewed individuality. For now they wore no uniforms, and the hair, ancient symbol of power, was growing freely again. They no longer resembled each other, and had lost their sole asset in camp, comradeship. They looked just like everyone else, and had to cope just like everyone else, though they did not have the same inner resources.

So it is, in all of these circumstances, camp survivors' experience has exact parallels with survivors of incest and sexual abuse. We are damaged physically, emotionally and intellectually.

The chances of internal injury are high in a young victim, and pregnancy is an ever-present possibility once the victim has reached puberty. But even without any of these obvious risks, gynaecological problems are more common than not, increasing our feelings of fear and self-disgust. Any disturbance in menstrual cycle is a constant reminder that there is something different and wrong about us, something that has to do with our sexuality. The question of our sexual identity is a threatening one. Through the media we are taught from the outside what we have never learned from the inside, how to be feminine. Appearance is confused with essence. We are encouraged to believe that womanliness is something that can be applied by judicious choice of clothes, perfume, make-up. In this way our bodies are divided into exterior aspect, which may or may not come up to standard, and interior experience of physical discomfort or pain, pain which often baffles gynaecologists, making us feel even more unreachably different. Being examined, applying medicaments, undergoing even minor operations, are harrowing ordeals which we postpone as long as possible. In such treatment, we relive the invasion of our

femininity. We cannot explain the need for patience, understanding or extra gentleness to the doctor. Indeed, because
such problems are so intractable without psychological
help, we often receive impatience and dismissal from doctors
frustrated in their attempts to cure us. I can recall a period
of high stress in my life when I was visiting a gynaecologist
and a psychiatrist on alternate weeks, neither of whom
knew of the other's work with me. I myself did not make
the connection at the time, but felt only that I was an
inexplicable oddity and nuisance to both of them. The loss
of femininity is not confined to our bodies, but extends to
our sexual relationships, should they be at all possible.

We have not only lost security in womanliness. We have
lost the security of alikeness to the rest of humanity. We
look like others from the outside, but much that is part of
our memories, our lives, is unmentionable in ordinary
conversation. The results of the abuse are also too difficult
to explain. We feel we have nothing in common with our
contemporaries. Whole chunks of ordinary experience are
missing and have to be improvised, to be bent to fit the
'norm', for we know the fact of being sexually abused will
be too much of a bombshell to drop into any conversation,
and we fear further degradation. Life is a continuous
struggle to decide whether we will be accepted even though
different, a long and painful learning that mostly we
are not.

We don't know what it is to be part of a giggling group
of teenagers, to go to discos, be frivolous, have fun, have
casual boyfriends, be fascinated with fashion, pin-ups, pop
music. Our love-life is nil, or we have one, over-intense long
term relationship, or we cannot cope with any but superficial, hardly-touching, fleeting friendships. Some of us need
physical cuddling so much that we are willing to trade sex
for it, since sex means nothing, so blanked-out with fear is
sexual feeling. Talking with acquaintances or colleagues at
work, we know that all this is different, that we have lost
our adolescence because we have never been able to enter it,

and that therefore we cannot be the same as other adults, and dare not reveal this too openly. This loss of solidarity with the rest of humanity is a loss more hurtful than even the original loss of innocence, because it is long drawn out, and has consequences every day of our lives. It is a position of isolation, freakishness. It is the intensification, over a lifetime, of the adolescent struggle to discover and preserve our identity at the same time as seeking what we have in common with others. It is an endless struggle, however, for it has to be carried out against great odds, not least of which is a cover of false assurance. It proceeds very slowly and cautiously, with many pitfalls and disasters, each of which teaches us to mistrust ourselves and others a little more.

In many ways we find it difficult to emerge from this sense of ourselves as not truly grown up. It is as if, on some plane within us, the frightened little girl is continuously crying desolately. For this reason, when asked to write as part of my therapy, it came most naturally to me to write in the present tense, to release her and allow her to speak. The confusion of child and adult identities was the confusion of past with present, and only after I was able to speak, and write of speaking about the abuse, did I become able to speak and write in the past tense. Till then the past was carried as an intrinsic part of the present, and could not be separated. But even after that, I had to be shown many times, in many ways, even specifically told in words that it would be all right to be grown up, that I could stand alone. And yet, as well as being adult-children, we have also known ourselves as child-adults, as older, more seasoned, tougher than most people. We are children, but we are children with ancient eyes, eyes that have looked upon literally unspeakable and frightful events, taking in knowledge that has left us permanently alienated. As children, adolescents and adults we look out upon a world full of people who seem able to relax and have fun. When we try and join them, we feel as if we are moving out of some inner world which is more real than the outer one, a world where life is serious and potentially grim, where time must not be wasted on banal trivia. Moving between inner and outer worlds causes a series of small, continual culture shocks, for each of the worlds seems unreal when in the other.

Intellectually we suffer also. I spent my schooldays in a dream, withdrawn, friendless, believing myself to be both stupid and lazy, though I was aware also of having a broader base of interest than most of my classmates, and knowing answers in my head that I did not have the initiative to put up my hand to say. At school I did not read until I was nine, though at home I was reading far in advance of my chronological age. No one noticed this dichotomy as my parents and teachers hardly ever communicated. I myself could not explain it, and simply lived with these two sets of abilities unquestioningly. Reading from a primer at school was an extremely tense affair, daily dreaded. Reading at home was an escape, almost a different activity, which it took me years to realise was not different.

In all subjects I came far behind the others throughout my schooldays, assuming the ignominious title 'bottom of the class' almost as an annual ritual at the end of each school year. Each day I would walk to my place, sit down and switch off my attention. I don't know what I thought about, but only that I spent years thinking about it. Often the boredom became painful, and I would make pictures for myself secretly by pressing my closed eyelids with my knuckles, very hard, causing fireworks to erupt in the darkness inside my head. Only once did I cause any comment by doing this, as my inner disturbance was making me rock in my chair so hard that I fell off it, and came to, surrounded by the laughter of classmates and the scornful irritation of the teacher.

While at school, I never seemed to be able to get together much concentration. Only after leaving school, when no one was expecting anything of me academically, did I allow my intelligence to struggle through, to assert itself enough to gather sufficient paper qualifications to get to college.

63

I was motivated by the realisation that if I didn't, I would be condemned to boredom forever. But even then, I minimised this belated success. I regarded it as a stroke of luck, rather than a result of my own hard work. I saw myself as incapable of any independent effort. Everything happened to me, and I could cause nothing. This feeling is very common among survivors. Our learning has been impaired, and we believe we cannot learn. Our experiences at school reinforce our belief, causing further disintegration as they do so. At the same time, we do not appreciate how much we have learned, only in another field, the field of survival, compared to which academic learning is an irrelevant luxury.

There are many unburied bodies, and each has to be checked for any sign of life. If I had been asked three years ago what sort of childhood I'd had, I would have thought of my unhappiness in terms of school, my shame in terms of what I was afraid was my innate stupidity. As therapy progressed, it was as if parts of me were stirring, showing signs of life. My intelligence was aroused and, because seen and taken for granted, began to work overtime, to make up for all the time spent hidden. I was revitalised physically, breathing altered, my whole muscular structure toned up. I felt healthy in a way I had never been able to count on. Emotionally, life speeded up to such an extent that I could hardly bear it. I swung between needing total distraction with people other than family, to needing time to be alone. Anything in between was almost intolerable, as I found it impossible to hide violent feelings surging within me for long. Weekends were especially difficult, as there wasn't enough of the necessary solitude, and I simply had to drive away from the house, to sit alone somewhere for two or three hours while thoughts and feelings raced through my head.

The extremely delicate work done with me had the effect of shaking me vigorously, insistently awake. I was told that

I alone would have to do the work of freeing myself, at a time when I had no idea what this could possibly mean. I didn't know that sitting in the car thinking and feeling was that work, that trusting was that work, that letting go tears and anger instead of keeping them in was that work. Or that the fear that made my stomach churn for days, kept me sleepless at nights, was only possible to bear because it was balanced by a confidence in the worker, a confidence that enabled me to take each difficult step towards her. This was my response to emotional touch, the way I showed that life still flickered in me, that I could be moved. Both figuratively and literally I slowly opened my eyes, eyes kept previously cast down when near any danger of being really looked into. And as I did so, I allowed my gaze to meet that of the worker, and saw that she wasn't hiding anything, saw complete openness and lack of fear. It was a revelation, one that had to be tested rigorously. I had believed that, were the truth known, everyone lived in a cage like me, and could only escape temporarily. I had believed that someone who worked with peoples' unhappinesses would need barriers even more than most, would need to hide behind status, uniform, label, technique or system, that no one could expose themselves to the risk of holding and feeling another's pain directly. I had not imagined it possible that anyone in that position could afford to understand me too clearly and yet see me as an ordinary person, as ordinary as they were. But it only made sense for me to be healed by being given respect, for that, above all, was what I had lost.

It was this attitude of respect, proceeding from self-respect, that conveyed itself to me in a million tiny ways, teaching me so much that I needed to know. It could not have been faked. The spontaneity of the worker's every movement, the exact tilt of her head, the language of her hands, of her tone, of her way of dressing, of decorating her room, all these spoke of her innermost intention and concern, for all these arose and were created out of her care. And this care was not only for me, but for herself. I could not have learned that I was worth caring for from one who did not celebrate her own worth. From this position of inner confidence, she could speak and act freely and flexibly, as if her job was a continuation of her own life's material, and not placed in a separate compartment for safety. Just by being like that, she was able to model the possibility for me, and to draw me from the cage I had shut myself into, the cage of my tense body, my rigid behaviour patterns, my past, my fear of living, the cage which had become a kind of safety.

Going up the stairs towards the little room where I knew it would be safe to come out of my imprisonment, if only temporarily, I would chat brightly about the weather, grumble about the effect of so many stairs on my leg muscles, compliment the worker on her dress, or maintain a scared silence. I got to know what was coming and what it would feel like three minutes after I was seated opposite her in her room. Something in me would start to fall, as if a voice had called 'Going down' I would experience the terror of it, the exhilaration of it. After a few times I got to look forward to the sensation. I came to trust that if need be, she would catch me, she would not let my precious dignity be broken. And so at times I would become aware of my existence in a new way. I would suddenly notice that my arms and hands, legs and feet, would be sprawled awkwardly, anyhow, like the collapsed bars of a deserted cage. My body was not needed, instead I would be sweating with the intense effort of dealing directly with my emotions, an exercise I was wholly unused to, having spent a lifetime avoiding it. I was working hard, and no one could have prepared me for the nature of that work. At last I had let go my tight grip on myself, and only the repeated taking of this risk enabled me to realise that the bars of the cage that imprisoned me were my own fingers.

A Kind of Safety

My fingers
and the ledge they cling to
atrophy.

My eyes weary with gazing
only at the live green moss
wedged in this crevise before me.

Once
to justify the beauty
of this tuft
I called down
to the abyss
the news about the moss
and
just briefly
dared to glance below.

Lush lay the valley.
Thick grasses awaited my bare toes
and every moss on every tree
oozed moisture and small swift insects.

My fingers clutch convulsively again
leaving the fossil of scratch marks
petrified.

PART 4

Cry Hard and Swim

The rug was small, oval, blue-patterned with flowers, edged with a fringe. My eyes travelled round and round its perimeter, studied its pattern, tried to straighten by the sheer intensity of their gaze the fringe which was never straight. Sunlight lay on the rug sometimes, lay on the feet which faced me from the other side of the rug. A woman's feet, always elegantly shod. A woman's voice reaching out to me. Talk was easy at first, pleasant, sociable. Then somehow, I never figured out how exactly, it was difficult, immensely difficult. Long pauses, me struggling to answer, struggling with one of her answers, with the layers and layers of significance packed into each minute. I was worried about my child. 'Children always know when they are loved', the voice said. 'Then why didn't I?', I asked, and couldn't hear the answer, because already it was slamming all round my skull with incredible violence. My own answer to my own question.

Tall grass, so tall it must mean I am very small. Planting bulbs in the oval flower bed, bulbs that would grow into scillas, little blue flowers. If the bulbs were planted in a pattern, I would see it emerge in colour in the spring, in the colour of my eyes. And here it was, many springtimes later, the pattern my grown-up eyes were tracing, vivid in the spring sunshine. Only it was not out in the garden. It was inside, in the room with this woman. She was making me look at it. Or was it that I could not stop looking at it, could not take my eyes from it to look at her? I had been watching it in secret, planted inside me for so long. Then, suddenly, within minutes of being with this woman, it lay between us, the pattern of my childhood. And somehow I forgot how to be sociable, how important good manners were. The only thing that mattered was examining that pattern, getting it out between us, deciphering its intricate connections, how it all fitted together. She was there, that was all I knew. In some way, she made it possible to see. I could not see her yet. I could not look at her, not when the pattern was so visible. What I saw when I looked at it made me know myself to be fragmented, ready to shatter, aware of the utter exhaustion of holding myself together.

Once, she asked me if I found it difficult to look at her. And I managed to shoot a single glance at her for a second, an instant that dazzled my eyes, that hurt my inner eyes. So difficult to face another human being across that pattern. She was so far away from me, and yet to meet her eyes was to suddenly reduce the distance to unbearable closeness. Unbearable to be so close to another person, one to whom the pattern was also visible. If I looked at her again, I might have to speak of it, to acknowledge its presence openly, to acknowledge my brokenheartedness, to hear again the voice, the real voice with the real words, drawing my eyes to hers, from pattern to person, from my life's rigid arrangement to the person that was Eve.

'We are here to talk about your life. You may die next year, or you may still be alive in fifty years. It is your life that is important, now, here, in this room.'

Eve leaned forward as she spoke these words, looking directly into my eyes and cupping her hands between us as she talked, as if holding something of priceless value. My life?

My life was a wash-out, a pointless, relentless, daily struggle. I was a hopeless mother, but I was afraid to go back to work. My marriage was very difficult, but separation was unthinkable as I could not survive alone. Everything I had ever taken on, cared for, striven for, had come to disillusionment. Now it was as if each sphere of thought or activity was a reminder of ignominious failure. The best thing about my life was that no one knew how desperately miserable I was. For a long time I had managed to keep everything under control, at least in public.

As a child I had come to judge just how close I could walk to the other girls in school, close enough to hide the embarrassing fact that I was always alone, apart enough to avoid having the difference between them and me emerge painfully once more, in schoolgirl conversation, as I failed once again to achieve what appeared to be normality. I was too serious, yet too stupid, too intense, yet chronically absent-minded. I couldn't do my work and I didn't know how to play. But as I sat facing Eve most of a lifetime later, looking at those cupped hands of hers, it seemed that she, at any rate, thought she was holding a life of infinite promise. She was speaking of the future, the future where I was going to be living the rest of my life. By dealing with what had gone before, the future was going to be possible. Not dealing with it had not made me wish to kill myself, but nonetheless I did not wish to live.

Looking at Eve holding my worthless life, inviting me to share my loneliness with her instead of guarding it in such a self-defeating way, I wondered how it would be not to pretend any longer, and what that surrender would cost me. There was a choice here. I could move away, try to accept the fact that I was different, walk alone for the rest of my life. Or I could approach and walk with Eve, just for an hour every week, taking the risk of discovering once and for all that nothing would ever work.

I didn't want to know that for sure, but even then, I knew that whatever emerged during my journey with Eve, whether it was good or bad news, I would know it for sure. Eve was making a definite shape with her hands, but what the shape contained was invisible. All that was visible was her hands. I looked at them and I saw that they were strong hands, used to hard, practical work. They wore two rings, the plain wedding ring, symbolising faithfulness, the jewelled engagement ring, sparkling, symbolising joy. Everything about her held meaning, but what was important to me as I sat there trying to decide whether to trust her or not, was whether she was a happy person in herself. I knew that if she was at heart a troubled person, the promise she was holding out to me was a false one, and when it came to the crunch (whatever that would be), she would not be able to deliver.

Survivors are hungry children, wandering lost in the tangled wood of adulthood, who sometimes come across a house made of sweets, a promise of something to eat at last. They know there is someone within, but they have to decide whether it is a good fairy or a witch, and with the shrewd eyesight of children, they do.

The way they do it is to look at the person within to see if she is hungry too. Everyone has needs, the need for intimacy to dispel loneliness, the need for recognition and esteem, the need for power, the need to be needed. What the survivor is assessing through her child's eyes is whether those needs in the worker are being met elsewhere, or whether she, the survivor, will be expected to meet them in some way. If it is the latter, then the worker is a witch, an eater of hapless children. If the former, the worker has real food to spare, and has it in abundance.

Eve demonstrated quite concretely that she was not hungry. When she came to my house, as she did sometimes to work with my marriage or my family, she would accept only tea, never anything to eat. This disappointed and worried me vaguely. Sometimes she would stay a long time, and I knew she didn't eat much midday, and must be very hungry. When I asked her about it she made light of it. I found myself growing more and more anxious for her, and, much to my surprise, for myself.

One day I sat down and figured out why I was so nervous. With my mother I had had an understanding, an unspoken deal. I was to look after her, and she would look after me. This meant that she would worry about me, which was her way of demonstrating care. That it also demonstrated lack of trust in my ability was the price I had to pay for the care I craved so much from her. Eve had a different deal, expressed quite openly. 'I will look after myself, and you look after yourself', she would say whenever I worried about causing her bother, keeping her hungry, keeping her

74

late. It took me a long time to accept that she left when she chose to leave. I was used to the idea that love and attention have to be bargained for. Since my mother drove a very hard bargain, I couldn't believe that all this care was really free. Yet each week, for a solid hour, I had her total attention and understanding, and felt the care coming through.

One evening, as I was leaving the clinic after a particularly challenging, gruelling session, which had taxed my powers of concentration to the limit, she gave me a big smile and said, 'Now, I'm going home to watch the Cup Final.'

What was it about this statement, extraordinary in its ordinariness, that sent me moonwalking down the road, my feet bouncing off the pavement as if untrammelled by gravity? It wasn't just what was, to me, the comical incongruity of someone of Eve's finely tuned sensitivity turning out to be a football supporter. It was that at last I had, in full, all the elements I needed to isolate the solution to the puzzle about what Eve expected of me.

Eve cared about me. But Eve was not going home to worry about me. Far from it. She was going home to enjoy her life in her own way. Yet during that session we had brought to light some issues that worried me extremely, without any apparent solutions. Then what was this tremendous relief I felt, this mad desire to run all the way home, laughing and singing?

What she was telling me was that she would look after herself. I had no responsibility for her. What she was telling me was I would, I could look after myself. She at any rate trusted my ability to do so, even when I did not. What she was telling me was that she was no hungry witch. Her needs were being met in her own private life, and she didn't need me, didn't depend on me, didn't want me to depend on her, expected nothing but that I should give my utmost to the work we were doing together.

What she was offering was her faith in my ability to make it, a faith that was not subject to, but resulted in that capacity to enjoy life which made her belief in me credible. This was what she had been holding out to me in her cupped hands, right from the start. This was what encouraged me to give space to every paradox with which she presented me by word and example from then on.

Her wish for me was that I would become able to hold the integrity of my life, past, present and future, with as much respect for its intrinsic and unique value as she had when holding it. There was no catch, no unspoken deal, no conditional caring, no apologies for the cliché that life is worth living. It was so simply obvious to her, and so irresistibly spontaneous was her gesture to illustrate it, that from the very start, watching her hands, I sensed the beginning of that curiosity which, even in the smallest baby, is worth celebrating as the sign of a positive interest in being alive.

Journey

My footsteps tread this fenceless field of snow,
but I don't know where they might lead,
I haven't been there yet,
and I forget where they began.

This being so,
you do not seek to bind me with a sigh,
for you were the first to bring to bear in mind
where feet might go,
and freely you invite me with your joy,

knowing you can draw me only when I yield,
deep into the blinding white with you.

Awakening

Ghosts go
gradually,
First, by glow of morning star,
they stir
uneasily,
sensing their answers
questioned.

Sleepers wake
drowsily,
lifting their heads
to see if time to rise
has come.
Then
when eyes meet
in the dawn of understanding
ghosts go,
dwindling,
as, with a stretch
and sleepy yawn,
I will take more of you
and you of me
in daylight, slowly.
For we awake to flesh our love
with what we have kept from death,
and take from morning touch of lovers
all that is left to grow
when ghosts have gone
from day's deep
breath.

It was not until after she had gone that I found out the first name of my therapist, and it was as if a piece of jigsaw that was vital to the picture slipped neatly into place. Her name was Eve, and she was the third Eve in my life. Third time lucky.

The first Eve had been the nursemaid who briefly became my father's mistress for a disastrous few months. I never knew her, scarcely even knew of her. Yet her existence in the house before my birth cast a long shadow over my early years, and the tone of the few dark phrases that were whispered of her, just once in all my childhood, was such that we knew her to be the wickedest, dirtiest slut alive, and that what she had done (though unspecified) put her outside the pale of human consideration or contemplation.

The second Eve had been my godmother, and a perfect lady. She was the wife of a diplomat, and my mother always spoke of her with an admiration bordering on awe. Because they travelled abroad so much, I only saw my godparents a few times during my childhood, but their arrival was always the signal for great excitement and huge preparations of hospitality. My mother used my Aunt Eve, as we called her, to show me what a real lady was. A genuine lady knew the quality of things, could choose anything correctly, from well-made clothes to well-made servants. A genuine lady could run a banquet for a hundred people without any fuss or panic, because a genuine lady always maintained her calm and gracious exterior.

These two examples made a formidable combination of model for my mother to use in her teaching about sex. Not that we ever discussed sex, but I knew that nothing my godmother did could be faulted. So it struck me all the more forcefully that the one and only time I saw my godmother lose her cool was when she found me sitting in the bath, while my brother, who was two years older than me, peacefully urinated at the lavatory. Entering the bathroom like a whirlwind, she denounced my poor brother in withering tones, declaring him not to be a gentleman (which was

78

true), or modest (which was most ironically untrue). Topping this off with the ultimate threat that she would inform our parents, she swept out, propelling a perplexed David before her. I never heard any more of it, but remember getting out of the bath to lock the door, getting dried and dressed hurriedly, eager to cover my five-year-old shame as quickly as possible. This was my mother's best friend. This was a genuine lady.

Going back to one of the many days of lost innocence to draw out one example of the deceptions of my childhood helps to realise how, even then, it had started − the desperate attempt to sort out the genuine from the false. When, nine years later, I started to lie in a way that must have been ludicrously obvious to everyone around me, I think perhaps I was giving up the struggle. The stress of my father's approaching death was too much for me to maintain the search for truth any more. Or maybe lying so constantly and outrageously was merely an alternative way of searching for the truth. Of searching for the limit where someone would stop me, where someone would tell me, if not what was true, then at least what was definitely untrue.

Eve. To discover that her name was Eve. To me, till then, her most important name had been 'you'. Yet at the beginning and end of each session, we had addressed each other in friendly but formal fashion, and I knew this had to be, although I didn't wish it, and it always startled me when, at the end of some intimate and intricate hour, she used my married name, and thus required that I use hers.

But this was the discipline within which we worked, the discipline of reality. I was a wife and mother, this was the present day, and at the end of it, I had to go home and make the tea. She opened me out, helped me to see what was inside me, take it all to bits to see which were useful to me in the present, and which were useless, heavy and disposable. She could speak to the child in me, reaching right through the wife and mother, through the adult I had become, through the adolescent, with all its questions, to the child, transfixed with fear. This was 'you and I' work. And at the end of it, she had to bring me back up through all those levels again, and send me home a functioning adult. I never left her without her using my formal name once, setting me back on my feet. And as I walked home again with my children, I was conscious that my very way of walking was changing, that my back was straighter, that I was holding my head more erectly. She had taken me apart, but each time she did so, she joined me up again, binding all the levels together and sealing them with this 'Mrs', as if to emphasise the reality of my present responsibility. It is a lovely and dignified thing to be able to take the reins of responsibility into one's own hands, to accept commitments and honour them if at all possible, and it was by simple dint of using my formal married name that she conveyed her confidence that I could. The mere certainty of her respect for me, despite my awkward negotiations with life in the present and past, joined me up, healed me, drew me more and more into a reality I had become too frightened to move in.

Eve — 'life'. Her name speaks of what she was to me. Her most penetrating message, the one that I seized upon with amazement over and over again, was 'you may'. May is spring, new life, new possibility. Eve was the permission-giver, the introduction to freedom, the freedom to be exactly what I am without fear.

My fear was physical as well as emotional. The one aspect displayed the symptoms of the other's difficulty in functioning. And yet I was almost unaware of fear, except in the primitive times-off that were becoming more and more frequent, and in dreams and poems. Mostly I experienced it as the deadness of boredom, the boredom that is one of fear's many masks.

Shortly after my therapy began, I started to have a totally unexpected reaction physically, so unexpected that for a long time I made no connection between the two. Half a dozen times a day, my body would suddenly jerk uncontrollably, as if for a second my whole insides crumpled and reformed. It was noticeable to no one but myself, but it puzzled and worried me, because I had never heard of such a phenomenon. I took the problem to my GP, who explained it as an anxiety reaction. But that was not how it felt to me.

Trying to express it to myself later, the image came to me of icebergs breaking away from distant wastes of ice, sliding into the sea with a crashing, crackling sound. It was happening in some remote place where everything was white, still, silent, and somehow, for some reason, I, going about my housewife's day, was being enabled to sense it happening from afar. Only it was not in fact a distant place at all. It was happening within my own body. And this was how I came to know how far away, how estranged I had been from my own body. After that I no longer worried about the strange symptom, because I understood what the signs meant and welcomed them. I also understood that the GP was right. As every adolescent knows, discovering sexual feelings for the first time causes as much confusion and anxiety as joy and wonder. I was just a late developer!

Eve. How did she manage to get through to me in this delicate area? How did she manage to reverse the message of the first two Eves, and in so doing, to reverse the spell their existence had cast on me? Eve number one was a tramp. Even my father would have called her that, and my mother did not have to. Eve number two was a lady. She obeyed instinctively the rule which said a lady ought to ignore everything sexual. For me, she contained in the phrase 'not nice' the implication 'disgusting', and therefore, 'terrifying'. But I had to re-examine this assumption with Eve number three, because she wasn't afraid of handling the topic of sex. She was comfortable with her own sexuality, and at the same time, in my parents' terms, she was a lady. This was a combination my father and mother, each in their extreme and opposite ways, had impressed upon me as utterly incompatible. Yet just the contact, over a period of time, with the living proof that these factors were perfectly compatible, affected not only my thinking processes, but far more importantly, my emotional and even physical ones.

It was not that she talked exhaustively on the subject, or imposed her own life style or opinions, or probed to find out what was troubling me. She simply provided a secure atmosphere in which I could, when ready, ask my questions. Anything more would have scared me off. But in this atmosphere, I gradually became less and less scared, and was eventually able to ask outright for sex information, whereas at first I had defended myself by a veneer of sexual sophistication. My naivety had remained unaffected by attempts to read various sex manuals. This was rather like reading a travel guide to a country I was intending to visit, but had no means of getting to. To be with Eve was like being with a native of that country, someone who would, if and when I asked, be willing to describe it for me. The easy and straightforward manner of her description was as important as the description itself in convincing me that this country was available for me too. No book can compare to the power of the human voice in conveying such a possibility to a survivor. And yet, enormous as the implications of this possibility were, I tried to appear to receive her few word-seeds as naturally as she spoke them, not to show a sign that they meant anything special to me. But inside, everything suddenly turned golden-warm and sunshiny, and I was filled with amazed delight.

Eve was not a sex therapist. She was a social worker. But she was able to prepare the way for me to be able to realise my need for sex therapy, and to ask for it when the time came. She was able to direct me to where I could get it. Eve was the end of my search for an acceptably sexual way to be. She was a genuine person, and in being so, she allowed me to be too.

Sea Creatures

A sunlit afternoon
is not the ideal time
to hunt for jewelled sea creatures
in amongst the gloom
of sea-bed ferns.
Conditions for their capture
must be learned by rote,
for they demand
that all be dark and still,
that boats be drawn in to shore,
that men should gather at the bar
for fishing lore, and women play
madonna, queen or whore.

But you and I, love, floating
in our sun-silked room,
caress our rippling cat to frenzy
till, with flash of sea-jewel eyes,
he leaps the open window
leaving us alone
and drowning
deep.

MOTHERHOOD

For Mark, becoming a separate person

Crosslegged at twelve
I found you
sitting in the midnight silence
struggling with your thoughts.

Shakily you stood up
as I came in,
pretending it wasn't happening,
you, who never have problems.

Then out they came
limping from your lips.
'Is this the way it's going to be
from now?' you asked.

My heart turned over, arms
aching to hold you,
and in a word, I did,
with my eventual
'yes'.

Held you
at the distance of our years
curved in the closeness
of our mutual dilemma.

In spite of a long, difficult and heavily drugged labour, cul-
minating in the birth of my first son, Mark, I could not sleep.
The ward was dim, the pale humped shape of each mother lay
still beside the transparent perspex cradles, each enclosing a
new miracle, a new person. I lay round-eyed in the dark, and
refused the sleeping pills offered by the nurse. I didn't want
to sleep, to waste this feeling, this night of glittering bliss.
I wanted her to stay, share my wonder at what was all around
us, the wonder of this profound transformation of my body
and mind, the wonder of my new son. But she left, and I lay
alone, sensing how the great hospital stretched out in the
darkness all around me, filled with sick patients and pain,
maybe worse pain than I'd experienced in labour, but bringing nothing to birth. Only we, the privileged few in the
maternity ward, were thus blessed at the end of our suffering.
Great suffering, and a great blessing.

I thought of my perfect son, peaceful by my side. In the

morning I was going to know. In the morning I would lift him and look into his eyes, and I would know at last what love was. All mothers loved their children. From my love for Mark, all other loves could now be measured. Now I could find out if it was possible for me to love. To have my own baby, to have full permission to love someone so unthreatening as much as I wanted to, without any doubts as to the rightness of this, seemed a reward that I could never have hoped for, a chance to be someone, someone very important at last, if only to one baby.

How many defeats make one surrender? In thirteen years I had become tired, guilty, resentful and had resoundingly failed as a mother. I had three lovely children, and everything was going wrong. I knew they weren't happy, and I knew it was my fault, must be my fault. Thirteen years since Mark's birth, eleven since Steven's, three since Frances slipped, feet first, on to the delivery table. Time had not shown me what love was. Time had only confused me, so that I didn't know whether I loved them or whether the primitiveness of my emotion towards them amounted to possessiveness. I only knew that I was exhausted, that I yearned most of all to lie down and sleep the clock round and round and round, but my duty as a mother wouldn't let me. I had been a 'good mother'. I had bought only educational toys, calculated the best nutrition, read books to my children endlessly, taken them to every interesting outing for miles around. I had tried never to smack them, and mostly succeeded. But in spite of all the primary-coloured toys, I couldn't play with them. I could hardly speak to them. Most of my words came out of the story books we read together. I couldn't concentrate long enough to sustain a conversation with my children, couldn't listen to them. I needed to be in my world of silent thoughts, my world that I had never learned how to share.

And yet they worried me so much. The boys' rivalry for my attention tore me in two. I felt all their unhappiness, added it to mine, and longed impotently to make us a happy family, the kind they show cricketing at the seaside on holiday brochures.

Believing in happy families was like believing in fairies. I had always been sceptical of anyone who laid claim to a happy family life, had always been on the lookout to pinpoint the untruth, the self-deception in such a claim. I needed not to believe in real family happiness, to protect myself against being duped twice. But I also needed to believe in the possibility for my own children, to try for it endlessly, dashing myself against the ideal until I broke, gave up, lay down and slept for longer and longer periods, to protect myself against the knowledge of my failure as a mother, my failure to love enough.

Frances. A girl. I laughed aloud as she was born, to the surprised amusement of a packed audience of nurses, students and other assorted bodies, all gathered to observe the difficult breech birth. A girl. A little girl, as I had been a little girl. Frances was my chance to start again, begin from the beginning, and this time get everything right. She would want for nothing, and nothing would be too good for her. But she would not be spoiled. I would teach her to use her brain, to be competent in many skills, to be strong and independent. But most of all I would teach her that she was deeply loved and respected. Already I respected the intelligence in the hawk-eyes gazing intently into mine as I held her, covered in blood and vernix, wrapped in sterile cloth. Frances would have everything that I had not had. Most of all, she would have my full attention. She would be the centre of my world.

But she could not be. Instead of being torn two ways, now I was torn three ways. In trying to resolve this, I told myself that Frances, being the youngest, needed me most, and thus managed to assuage some of the guilt of my almost total preoccupation with her. Developing her intelligence through stimulation in every possible way became my daily raison d'être. Her intelligence would be a weapon against her being hurt. Of course she would be hurt, no matter how I tried to protect her, but her intelligence would gain compensations for her that would be a buffer against deep hurt.

But Frances as she grew, rejected my attempts to teach her. She would turn away, would actually run away, when I even started. She did, however, want me to play with her, to talk to her naturally, to have fun with her. But I could not allow myself to have fun. I did not begin to know how to have fun. I did not know because, unwittingly, I had been living with grief since I was her age.

Frances sat on my knee in the clinic playroom, glaring at Eve. 'If looks could kill . . .' I murmured apologetically, for I had never seen such concentrated baleful antagonism on Frances' face before. Eve looked steadily back, explaining to Frances that we were going to chat, and that Frances must not interrupt. Did she not remember she had agreed not to interrupt? I held her very tight, so that she would know I loved her, then set her down to play again. I was in deep waters with Eve, and my distress had signalled itself to Frances. Although she had seemed to be quietly playing, she had an almost telepathic awareness of my state of mind.

I had been surprised and almost offended when Eve had very firmly, very courteously, asked Frances not to interrupt us, even though Frances for the most part complied willingly, at the clinic. Normally, she would not have allowed me five minutes to myself, and it was reaching the stage where her demands for my non-teaching attention were exhausting me, filling me with resentment, self-reproach and despair. I had planned all along not to send her to school, but to keep her at home and educate her myself. However, I knew that I was in no fit state to do this and dreaded becoming the very source of unhappiness I was determined to protect her from.

But it was in working with Eve in my own home that I

began to grasp how much my fears for Frances, the echoes of my own childhood fears, had dangerously unbalanced the family's equilibrium. For in her own home, Frances felt free to interrupt the family therapy sessions constantly, making them very difficult to continue. I felt I had to cater to Frances' need, and allowed her to disrupt the conversation, watching to see what Eve was going to do about this. Finally Eve asked the two boys if they didn't mind all these constant interruptions by Frances. I was flabbergasted at her forthrightness, which I would have called rudeness in anyone else. No one was allowed to criticise Frances. But even I could hear how very hesitantly, diffidently but definitely the boys answered yes, and how their hesitancy, their diffidence developed into deep resentment when she encouraged them to say more.

Eve was lifting a weight off everyone in this session. Without forcing me into the position of having to admit to my own impasse with Frances, which I would have translated as verging on rejection, for which I would not have been able to forgive myself, Eve showed me that I had been expecting the impossible of myself and the rest of the family.

Young as he was, Steven had all along sensed how much of my secret self I had invested in Frances, how urgently I needed to treat her as a little princess, though it was exhausting me. He had taken on responsibility for my needs, just as I had done for my own mother. But my necessity appeared to him to have priority over his need for a share of my attention too, so he could only 'ask' for it furtively, by getting into fierce fights in school, which had the dual effect of expressing his anger at the whole situation, and forcing me to pay attention to him. Yet when I or his teachers tried to talk to him about it he 'froze', his eyes went blank and he withdrew into himself, unable to express his predicament even to himself.

Mark had found a way to manage the situation without going under, by always being very good. Just entering adolescence, he was intensely concerned not to be childish, and he translated this as never complaining, or causing any bother.

Eve was allowing, encouraging both of them to complain openly, getting us to listen without feeling attacked, limiting Frances' demands, giving Frances the protection of adult-decided limits, and showing me that no catastrophe would happen if Frances took up a much reduced amount of attention. She was also beginning to give me a way to lessen my self-imposed exhaustion and stop being a martyr, thus forestalling endlessly rebounding resentment for the years to come.

This was the beginning of a very long process whereby we were enabled to learn how to allow all of our needs to be spoken clearly, so that they could begin to be met. In that this was new learning, I could see, after a while, how my childhood had lacked any natural opportunity for absorbing this ease of communication. Coming at the time when they did, when many of our ways of thinking and acting were about to come under scrutiny, question and criticism by our older children as they became adolescent, the new ways of becoming alive to each other saved us endless future pain and alienation. All this made clear to me, over time, how far off the mark had been my picture of a 'happy family', static in its little frame in my mind. I had expected it to happen magically, having no idea how to bring it about, or even that it could be brought about, given the right conditions, the freedom to feel and speak, the freedom to differ, the freedom to be a separate person with separate interpretations and needs. Over a long time the family became conscious of the growth within itself, and my husband and I had to grow with it, balancing our own needs as parents and individuals with the needs of our children for increasing independence within the security of the family. I discovered at first hand the natural happiness, confidence and love of children, ready to bubble up at any time, if they are only not buried

under the pressures of guilt, sadness and unspoken griev-
ances.

Little by little, Frances gave up her efforts to distract me
from my inner world, for that is how I came to see her
demands. Her attempts to comfort me by playing with me
became unnecessary as I emerged slowly into reality, and
became able to see her as a distinct little person in her own
right, and not a duplicate of myself. At the end of each
family session, she would bring me the drawings which
became her way of expressing her three-year-old viewpoint.
They showed that she had a very acute observation of
people and events, and could understand with revealing
accuracy what was going on. She came to demonstrate a
healthy self-sufficiency and assertion, although allowing the
family discussions to proceed. I remember the first time she
was quiet most of the way through, her sudden interpola-
tion among the polite leavetakings, as we all rose to say
goodbye to Eve. Somersaulting her way through the five of
us, she landed right-side-up, shouting, 'I matter too!' 'You
better believe it!' said Eve, and I knew she meant it for each
of us. For in myself, I was beginning to do so.

Family Therapist

Sculptress
working with this cube of stone
within which, petrified,
five statues stand, familiar
yet estranged.

Aware we're in here,
you don't chisel,
change us to a shape
of your imagining or will,

90

preferring to uncover us —
'What love can ask
is more than fear demands.'*

Thus stone crumbles,
and we become unstill, discovering
through your strength of hand
ourselves,
each other,
learning to breathe deep
and moving in and on and out
to new unknowns.

CLARITY

A Book Called 'Depression'

Can't eat it,
this thick paper sandwich,
can't get it down at all.

All I know
is my own story,
how, through the glass door
I look in at the child
who locked me out,
gesticulating, telling funny jokes,
anecdotes, singing songs,
acting like crazy,
not worrying, not imagining,
not feeling the floor
under her soft bare feet,
not being her

---

* Karol Wojtyla.

so that she won't understand
how long
how long
she's been alone in there.

Playing peep-bo
round the storm doors
till help arrives.

Ever since I can remember I have never been able to let my
mind alone. I have read everything I could lay my hands on
about the human mind, both in the emotional sphere and in
the intellectual sphere, following with a great though
amateur interest most of the various schools of psychology,
taking from their theories and systems whatever was useful
to me at the time of reading. Useful for what? How could
learning theory, child development, brain function,
psychopathology, etc., possibly hold any use for me? Apart
from a brief spell at college when I was expected to know a
very few of these things in order to attain a teaching qualifi-
cation, there was never any official need for any of this
knowledge. I found very few people who felt inclined to
discuss these things with me, yet it was such a strong need
in me to follow this private track that when Eve asked me
please to stop reading these kinds of books and I tried to, it
was so difficult at first that I realised it had become almost
an addiction. I was constantly drawn to pursuing my own
lines of enquiry, as if there was some enormously significant
quarry to be gained at the end of all this ceaseless search.
What was it? To myself I secretly named it discernment. But
in fact all this probing, like the probing of a sore tooth with
the tongue, was an instinctive seeking for recognition and
understanding, and with any luck, for self-healing of the
distress I was holding inside.

As all this vast store of knowledge was pouring into me
year after year, I would occasionally let out from myself a

small yelp of pain, in the form of a poem. After writing each poem I would cry bitterly for a while, strange harsh tears of misery and despair. For a day or two, whoever came to the house had to see what I had written, if I thought they would be at all receptive. Usually the response was complete silence, and an uneasy change of subject. This I found enormously hurtful and bewildering, not realising that the people I was showing the poems to were also hurt and bewildered at the depth of suffering revealed in this seemingly even-tempered, capable friend, neighbour or acquaintance. I was showing them a total stranger when they thought they knew me. What neither of us realised was that I didn't know me. I had elaborate explanations for each poem that had very little to do with myself, but only fooled me. The force of feeling expressed at the actual moment of writing got disconnected and sealed into the paper, so that when I looked at it afterwards, I could not claim it as my own.

Later when I joined a writers' circle, I found it slightly more satisfying to have my poetry judged technically. I learned so much about what makes poetry work, and the meaning of its technical terms that for a long time afterwards, I was too hamstrung by these learnings to write another word. No one ever discussed content, and on this level my hunger was still unsatisfied. It was as if, on picking up a bottle on the beach, and discovering a desperate message inside, a lengthy discussion on the quality of the handwriting ensued. Gradually the explanation came to me that my work was a threat to anyone I showed it to, though I could hardly, at the same time, believe this seriously, as I thought myself incapable of influencing anyone, much less threatening them. Only once did someone, through a third person, give me any real feedback, and I did not see it for what it was. Apparently he had said I was very lucky to have a way to let out what I was feeling inside. I pondered this for a while, and then gave up. 'So what, anyway?' I shrugged, 'It doesn't achieve anything.' I never connected what I was putting out by writing with what I was taking in by reading. It was this lack of connection between knowing and feeling that was symptomatic of my general malaise.

In the course of time I came to know Eve, who touched my pain fleetingly. And after a while, quite suddenly, without any premeditation, my first poem for years emerged one day, within the space of time between serving a hot meal and calling the children to eat. It was addressed, 'To the therapist, bringing a parent into the waiting room . . .'. I had watched this happen the week before, while I was waiting for my appointment, watched the way a mother had sat where Eve left her with a few quiet words, her red skirt flaring out over the chair like a poppy, her face closed, as if stunned with grief. Unwittingly I saw myself in this woman, and debated long within myself as to whether to take the chance of letting Eve see the poem. In the end I decided to send it, because her reaction would give me the answer to so many things I needed to know about her, that it would be worth the risk of misunderstanding or rejection, as it would show me either a red or a green light. In a way, I felt almost sacrilegious to be using a poem as a test, and yet it was the perfect touchstone.

So there we sat in the playroom the following week, with the unexploded bomb which was my poem between us, and me intently watching the movement of every muscle in her face. The mere fact that she had brought it, and was clearly not going to ignore it, was hopeful. Then she started to talk about it, and the first thing she did was not to thank me for it. In not thanking me for it, she showed that she understood me to have spoken. I had spoken, and my words were to be responded to, not treated as a present, an object totally unconnected with me. That might be how I saw them, but it was not how she did.

She started to talk about the poem, and the fact that there was a lot of what she called 'material' in it. Material. No one had ever used that word in connection with poetry in my experience. This was puzzling, but also intriguing. In the next few minutes, as she went through the poem line by line, asking me to explain more and more what I was meaning, I began to see that not only was Eve no literary critic, but she had no interest in literary criticism, nor any shame in her lack of interest. On the other hand, she seemed to be intensely interested in me. And for that I forgave her apparent lack of technical appreciation, and tried to feel for the right plain words to describe the tightly bound package of violent emotion I had handed her, not making a very good job of this unfamiliar task, but at least making a beginning. I had never in my life been asked the meaning of one phrase in one poem. I had never in my life felt so cared for when someone took the trouble to ask me to decode and translate what I was saying, without fear of seeming ignorant, so that we could both understand together.

That was the last time that I took Frances and used the playroom as a place for therapy. From then on I wanted to work with Eve without distraction in her room, and the time for playing around was over.

Orpheus loses Eurydice to the underworld. He ceases to sing, and instead makes a long and perilous journey to the underworld to find her. He pleads with the god of the underworld for her release, and the god allows it, as long as Orpheus does not look at Eurydice underground. So he tries to lead her up from the underworld, but before they have reached the outside world, he cannot resist turning and looking at her, and she instantly vanishes. Orpheus returns to the surface, broken-hearted.

Broken heart, broken mind, broken spirit. It seems to me that each of us has two quite distinct ways of perceiving, with the heart and with the mind, subjectively and objectively, with feeling and with knowing. And the strong spirit is that in which these two ways of perceiving can be used together, flexibly, almost simultaneously, in order to make judgements, decisions, actions.

In my understanding of the ancient legend, Orpheus is

objective knowledge, Eurydice is subjective feeling. Each, though very much alive, is incomplete without the other. Therefore all judgements, decisions and actions made out of the incomplete perceptions of intellect alone, or emotion alone, are bound to be partial judgements, impulsive or compulsive decisions, and ultimately frustrating actions.

What is needed is a way to get Orpheus and Eurydice out into the open together, so that they can look at each other without Eurydice vanishing. In order for this to happen, for the feelings not to dissipate into thin air and forgetfulness, they have to be pinned down somehow. They have to be written, painted, acted out to witnesses, taped, or spoken out loud in the presence of another, who must be trustworthy and credible, for a survivor's self-doubt is such that she does not consider herself credible. The most useful ways of recording feeling are those which we can keep and refer to. Dream and insight diaries are invaluable, making a map of our journey, so that we don't lose sight of important landmarks, any of which may point the way for our next step.

When Eve sat down with me and brought to the surface what I had been trying to say about my feelings of pain and fragility, words spoken from underground, in the first poem I gave her, she was like one who, by being also present, confirms the frequent but lonely sighting of a ghost, the ghost of Eurydice. Eve's presence gave me the courage to face the ghost, make it materialise, and consciously recognise myself in it.

The presence of another human being is vital to the perception of a survivor at the beginning, because her ghost is bound to be extremely frightening. That is why Eurydice disappears in the legend. Her appearance, although so necessary to Orpheus that he is compelled to seek her, is too terrifying to confront alone. In my mind she was always present, but never quite visible. She was visible to those with whom I had previously tried to share the poems, but because she appalled them into silence, I still could not see her.

Eve was the first to break the silence for me. Fearing the power of the poems to move the reader subjectively, I always made sure never to be present when Eve first read them. I was scared stiff that I might see her emotionally affected. Instinctively, I knew that for my recovery I needed her objectivity more than anything, as an aid to lend weight to mine temporarily, in order to balance the heaviness of what I experienced underworld.

Once Eve had helped to bring Eurydice up from the depths of my underworld, she did not continue to work with the poems, though I continued to write them. Over a lifetime, I had got into the way of thinking only intellectually, or only emotionally, and I had to achieve a better balance, practise the two ways of thinking together till they became almost simultaneous, so that my judgements would be more level, my decisions more realistic, and my actions more rewarding. For a year and a half I practised this with the help of Eve, other workers and finally alone, using simple everyday events, working individually, and in my roles as wife and mother. My husband and children were helped to accept the changing me, which was a labour of love for all concerned, as the accumulated misunderstandings, unspoken accusations and general rage flying around for years had put the family on a very precarious footing. We all had to change destructive habits and attitudes, and take on the difficult work of developing better ways of communicating. Gradually, life for all of us began to move more smoothly, or perhaps it was just that we became more able to weather the rough patches.

The way each individual in the family was listened to, each one's needs respected in the course of family therapy, not only taught each of us to do likewise, but made me feel cared for within my natural context, the one I had chosen and continued to choose, even after I had become strong enough in myself to choose otherwise. I was all the while

97

working on my own, constantly building new expectations of myself and my life in the light of each new insight. Battles with my husband and children over changing roles, attitudes, mutual understandings, might have split us as a family, if we had not had any guide to interpret what was being said, and help us consider it freshly. We were able to work together, rather than in spite of each other. There was both inner and outer disruption to heal, and each was given the chance to aid the other.

Having lived through this transformation with great wonder at the skill with which it was effected, I sometimes wish it had been available to my family when I was small. Then I remember how fiercely my father guarded the notion of the perfection of his family, his genius for charming and explaining his way out of tight corners, my own confusion in the midst of this cunning. Even if family therapy had been available, professional assessment of the likelihood of a successful outcome would have had to be extremely skilful and experienced. As well as this, the basic humility, the desire for change, perseverance, and the fundamental strength of goodwill necessary for real progress was lacking, as the damage inflicted by terror had gone too deep in each of us, including my father. Though my husband and I were also infected by fear, it did not have the same cause, but was mostly fear of the unknown, owing to lack of confidence in communication. But there was a deep motivation in each of us to continue as a family. We had more going for us than not, and were able to use the help offered to us well, though the process occurred almost imperceptively to us, and was slow and uphill work.

Ordinary events were the stuff of individual, marital and family therapy. They were treated just as Eve had treated the poetry. Together we decoded what was happening to find the attitudes which made things go wrong, or, after a while, right, and to catch the elusive feelings governing those attitudes. In fact I came to feel that I was daily walking through showers of poems, events, in everyday life that were haunted by Eurydice and coloured by her fear-filled aspect. Gradually they became more manageable, as I learned not to panic, but to pause and listen to my true feelings without outside help. I am still in the process of learning this.

As my feelings became more and more recognisable through continually being brought into the open, I came to live with them with increasing ease. Positive feelings arose to the surface when the weight of negative ones was lifted. With trust came spontaneity. Life became interesting and full of variety. I began to appreciate the other and delightful aspect of Eurydice, which is what motivates Orpheus to persist in seeking her to heal his heart. And it was only the clear-sighted acceptance of both Orpheus and Eurydice, of their joining together in daylight, that enabled me to heal mine.

Twirling tinily in the vastness of space, the earth glistened blue and white and unbelievably beautiful, like a child's ball, rolling across the slopes of an immense and limitless lawn. And the whole world gasped in wonder at this, the first photograph of our planet taken from right outside of itself, and yet by one of us, one of our own species, moved at the same moment to utter the ancient words of wonder – 'In the beginning was the Word: the Word was with God, and the Word was God.' In that moment space and time were suddenly related in a new dimension, creating a new and vibrant tension within which we were offered the chance to see ourselves from an entirely different perspective, to see our cosmic beauty, the beauty and fragility of our life, and to see this as a rare and precious gift which must not be squandered.

And so I sat down one day to try to bring forth a true image of my own genesis, not knowing how clearly and terribly the truth was going to emerge, not dreaming that I would ever find a way to manage all the anger, hurt and despair that flowed from my mind on to the paper in a stream of inky blackness, not realising that, in the act of writing, I was managing it, and better than I had ever been able to before.

This was my world. It belonged entirely to me. No one could criticise or minimise or dismiss it. No one could be horrified or hurt by it, for it was written only for my own eyes. No one could deny it, and most importantly I myself could never again try to deny it.

The casualness of Eve's suggestion that I write to my mother and keep what I write makes me tremble, to think that I might not have taken her up on it, might have dismissed the exercise as pointless. She never asked to see the letters, or suggested what might be written in them. This meant that I had no audience to write for, which had the effect of making the act of writing quite unselfconscious, with the result that I grew in consciousness of myself.

Much later I asked Eve why she had suggested writing to my mother, rather than my father. As she often did, she asked me to work it out for myself. And then I knew. I had been far angrier with my mother for the power she held and did not use, than I had been with my father, whose abuse of power was comparatively straightforward and understandable, even to a child, who knows what it is to be cruel, to pull the wings off butterflies and squash beetles. My mother not using her undoubted influence to save me, David or the other children, was a far more complex question, engendering a convoluted spiral of anger, guilt, scorn and pity, which constantly disappeared into its own centre whenever I tried to examine any aspect of it. In writing to my mother, I collected in one fell swoop the total amount of what I felt for both my parents.

Eve did not defend my mother. But she asked me to think about her, imagine what my mother's life must have been like. And after a long time, but not until after her death, I came to appreciate that my mother had given me everything that she could. It was not enough, but then my mother had not received enough either. What you don't have, you cannot give away. But my mother had wanted me to have everything that she considered important, and no parent can have a better intention.

When I had finished the letters relating to my childhood, and typed them out slowly with one finger, I spread them out on the carpet in front of me, and faced the impact of this new way of looking at my world. In doing so, I lifted myself from under its shifting, amorphous clouds, distanced myself, and gave myself permission to see. That world was now naked to view, stripped of all the cosy family myths which had up till now only confused me and hidden the source of my pain.

I made copies and presented them to Eve, but she hardly discussed them with me. I wanted her to say this cannot be true, to help me to deny it again. I wanted her to confirm it for me. But she left me to accept what belonged to me in my own time and in my own way. And it was not easy. Each day for months, I would re-read the letters, not knowing why I felt impelled to do this, but finding it impossible not to do so. Many times I wept bitterly while reading, my thoughts retracing the exact paths of my childhood. This time I could not close off the feelings when I put away the letters. I knew they were real, that they had come out of my own clear recollection. But as time went on, I felt less and less need to look at the letters. Slowly my defences against remembering lowered as I assimilated those feelings into consciousness, claimed them, and gathered together fragments of my life which had hitherto been too painful to touch, even with thought. Those months were a gradual process of the strengthening of emotional muscle, during which I learned to bear the truth without breaking down. In the first part of that time, my children often saw me in uncontrollable tears. My husband and I simply explained to them that I was reliving some painful memories, and that this might take some time. They seemed to understand this, and not worry too much, since we were able to talk about it, and they were not left in the dark. We all had a lot of support from the clinic at this time, and we were learning that it is safe to tell the truth to each other. Another new learning.

In the beginning was the word. I had wondered, after I first told Eve about being abused, what she was going to do about it. I waited a long time before it dawned on me that she was not going to do anything about it, that no one except me could do anything about it now. Eve could show me the way, but I was the only one who could choose to take that difficult way, and to shorten the road by the power of my own will to recover.

For me, words were the beginning, the beginning of learning to see. I saw myself from a different perspective, heard myself crying, felt the wetness of my tears, tasted their salt, and knew I was alive and not dead inside. When I let Eve see the letters, she spoke as if the child in the letters was not me, but a young girl who existed a long time ago. Her doing this helped me further to separate the present from the past which had possessed me as a dark and formless burden whose dead weight had been forcing me into a stooped position that I no longer had to continue to maintain.

As the woman I am, Eve did not offer me any facile sympathy. But her hands held and stroked the pages tenderly, as if I have given her something immeasurably precious, which must not be crushed or destroyed, and I experienced the very gesture as a healing, as if she was gently stroking away the tears from an invisible child's face.

Alice

> Was she surprised when,
> swimming in the pool of her own tears,
> she was swept with the waves,
> and all the other animals,

through the tiny door
into the beautiful garden,
key, table, food, drink and fears
forgotten, as in a dream?

I would have been surprised to find
the formula so simple –
'To find your own true size in tears,
cry hard and swim'.
The garden waits.

Health

It seemed to be taking a long time to get to the bank. Already I had been striding along for hours, and I was only a hundred yards away from my own home. What's more, moving seemed very difficult, as if I was wading thigh-deep through strongly incoming waves. Suddenly I stood still, sensing the approach of a tidal wave of panic which I knew would completely overtake me any moment, inescapably. I felt a burning heat rising up my chest, neck, face. Blushing furiously, terror-stricken, I tried to remember what was wrong, and knew all at once what it was. I had forgotten to dress properly that morning. Underneath my coat, I was naked. Hardly daring, but forced to, I glanced to check. Ah, thank God. It was all right. I was fully dressed. Perspiring now with relief, I battled on, wearily trying to remember the reason I was there. Oh yes, the bank. I started to think about my errand to the bank, imagining possible hitches to financial arrangements, reminding myself to write every-thing down as soon as possible afterwards. I was so terribly forgetful these days. Frighteningly forgetful. What was happening to me? Paralysed, I stopped in my tracks again, the tidal wave of panic sweeping over me, knowing for certain that underneath my coat I was naked. I had for-gotten to dress.

Anxiety is a very strange phenomenon. It is not one simple emotion, but a whole bag of emotions. Mainly it contains anger, the anger that a survivor has had to push down with ferocious energy as a child, through fear of its expression. I had seen for myself what happened when my father's anger was let loose on the family. I had seen the devastation anger could cause when allowed to let rip. I had also felt from my mother the vibration of repressed anger, though I never recognised it as such.

Never had I witnessed a constructive way of dealing with anger. Never had I seen my parents sit down and work out a problem together, or find any solution that did not involve someone getting hurt. Anger was an uncontrolled, capricious hurricane of terror that swept through the elegant rooms of our house leaving chaos and the fear of chaos in its wake. I learned to fear even the signs of impending anger, especially in myself. As a result I carried a mountain of volcanic fury that stuck hard inside me. The humiliation of sexual, physical and verbal abuse, the rigid family dogma, the emotional neglect of my mother, plus the constantly implicit responsibility of making things better for her, brought my little girl's indignation to boiling point and kept it there while I grew up. Fearing an explosion, I simply refused to acknowledge how angry I was. Because I had to forget the cause of fear, I had to have another reason for so much fear. I had none. I lived a very safe, suburban existence as a housewife and mother outwardly. Inside was where I really lived, in the soul, in the imagination. So that was where the fear showed itself and emerged quite irrationally in the outside world.

It was only when asked by a chance-met friend why I was carrying a crunched-up ball of paper around that I realised the extent of irrationality my fear had stretched to. I laughed, shrugged and threw it away, going back to retrieve it surreptitiously later, so no one would read the words, 'I am not naked', written on the paper. It was one of my gadgets for getting by. If I felt a panic coming on while I was out, I only had to squeeze the paper in my hand to reassure myself, without having to check, that I was not naked. That I did not think too hard about what I was doing was due to another huge fear of mine, the fear of insanity, the loss of control, the lapse into unreality. The ball of paper in my hand was reality, and I had to hang on to it desperately. I did not want to follow my brother David.

I might not have chosen this way of coping. There are many other ways, and they all have to do with retaining control, the control of the knowledge of anger. I felt very shaky inside, as if somewhere I could never stop trembling. My whole effort was geared towards controlling what happened to me, controlling the shakiness, the feelings of helplessness. By myself it could not be done, but the illusion of stability could be gained through marriage, by giving control of my destiny to another person, another situation. In this way, I chose when very young to avoid the danger of ever increasing the shakiness by making a wrong decision. But this non-decision was also a decision, a decision not to decide, to evade responsibility, since responsibility had been too heavy since childhood.

The ways of coping often combine comfort and punishment, experienced alternately. Some accident of fate might have shown me a way to comfort myself temporarily with alcohol or drugs. I might have made my protest using food, over-eating or starving myself into anorexia. I might have given control to luck, preferring the thrill and terror of gambling or shoplifting to the far more threatening underlying fear. I was drawn towards entering some stressful caring profession, for which I would have been ill-equipped. This way, I would have experienced and cared for my pain second-hand, through the pain of others, never having to directly confront my own, but achieving vicarious control, perhaps at others' expense. I might have unconsciously chosen a physically or sexually abusive man as a husband. This at least would have been a familiar demon, against whom I would have evolved ancient, if inefficient methods of defence and control. I would have seen anything which anaesthetised, or brought under even illusory control, the primitive fear of the inner explosion, as worth any problems which accompanied it. As it was, the fear was expressed in one of the many phobias it is possible to conceive, and no amount of logic was sufficient to subdue it.

The particular behaviour I was using to signal in a covert way my inner distress had not driven me into seeking medical help, for ten years earlier it had evinced itself in another form, with sufficient clarity to make me seek the help of a psychiatrist. I emerged from that experience unmoved, unchanged, and unwilling ever to try again. He had not even been able to touch my grief, let alone my rage, and I was left wondering at the end what my visits to him had been all about, relieved to be left alone, if not in peace.

A while after I had got to know Eve, I became aware that she was doing something to me and the something was to do with my mind. I decided I must be mentally ill, and screwed up enough courage to ask her the name of my illness, intending to go straight home and look it up to see how serious it was. Much to my indignation she declined to confirm my hunch, saying she didn't know, she wasn't a doctor.

I have always believed that if someone is ill they ought to be told, particularly if it is serious, and they have indicated that they want to know. But Eve wasn't telling me, and yet she was clearly working with my mind in some way or other. I could see she wasn't going to be tricked into revealing herself as the psychiatrist I was by now convinced she was, either. Indeed she plainly told me that she was not a psychiatrist. She was not even a psychiatric social worker. She was a generic social worker. She was an ordinary person, and so was I.

But this did not reassure me. I thought and thought how I could find out what was wrong, and finally hit upon the idea of going to my doctor. She couldn't refuse to communicate with him, and I would then demand to know from him what she had said.

It was almost with triumph that I next saw Eve, and was able to announce that I knew what was wrong with me, for the doctor had told me. I had a personality disorder, and medical opinion held it to be almost incurable.

There was a long moment's pause. I sat on the edge of my chair. Eve, with lowered eyelids, gazed at the floor meditatively. 'Do you not think,' she questioned softly at last, 'that we all have disordered personalities to some extent?'

We. That meant both of us. All of us. Everyone is bruised inside. Everyone has to struggle, needs help from others to reflect their innate goodness, despite the pain of the struggle. Everyone needs loving encouragement, not just me, not just me. She would not label me 'ill', nor allow anyone else to do so, particularly myself. If I was 'ill', then so was the rest of humankind. But I was not ill. I was just extremely and justifiably angry, and afraid to be so directly.

Eve was not concerned whether I got into a cupboard to scream, or needed to hold on to a piece of paper in order to go out, even though it was true that these things affected my happiness, and that of my family. Eve was concerned with what was causing this behaviour. The form of the behaviour was less important than what it was trying to express. By listening and responding to what I was saying through my behaviour, she dealt with the cause of it. As a result I no longer had any need to 'speak' in this way, and the behaviour ceased as the necessity for it diminished.

With Eve herself I had another way to introduce what I wanted to talk about at each session. I did it with clothes. At the beginning I turned up in my 'depressed' clothes, the brown jumper and saggy trousers I had worn almost constantly for all the preceding winter months. When I realised she was taking in what I was saying, I dressed for what I wanted to say, sometimes the adult in the smart suit, sometimes the child in tee shirt, sneakers and jeans. One day

I would dress as sleazily as a prostitute, wanting to tell her how I felt inside, the next day I would present myself in subtle, penitent shades of grey and soft brown, desiring her to forgive me for what I couldn't forgive myself. But she neither forgave me nor blamed me. She simply accepted what I said and dealt with it. She knew that she had no right to forgive me, and deep down, so did I. I would not have been able to accept her forgiveness as real, would have resented it bitterly as another patronising denial of my right to express the terrifying volcano of outrage simmering within.

Together we made the volcano erupt, I, through writing, talking, realising, she, through surrounding me with the complete reassurance that it was safe to do so, that she was not afraid of my anger, that I could not harm her, myself, or my mother, who was still alive at the time. My mother never saw the writing or heard me talk. She never actually felt the impact of my fury, because it was released symbolically, though nonetheless really. Otherwise I might have afterwards experienced a true guilt, which is even worse than a fake one.

It was Eve whose strength held me while I for the first time tested my own to the limit. And later, when the anger with my parents had torn through me with elemental force and abated, she was there waiting when it shifted to my husband, on account of the many misunderstandings and unspoken assumptions that fear and inability to communicate had accumulated. It was Eve who, all through, taught me the difference between assertion and aggression. She would not allow me to deny the truth that I loved my husband on the one hand, or the equal truth that I was very angry with him, on the other. But she showed me that love does not have to exclude anger, but that each can contain and transform the other, and that only fear can prevent this.

Later still, I learned from other workers how to control and direct anger, mechanically at first, awkwardly, and with many setbacks. Over the next year it became more natural, but will never be effortless. For it is this very effort, the effort of transformation, that is the stuff of which love is nourished, from which it grows, ripening like a fruit-bearing tree.

On the last formal occasion when I met with Eve, as she got up to go, she asked me always to remember that I had never been abnormal. On the contrary, my behaviour had been a normal response to abnormal circumstances, circumstances so harshly oppressive that I had been unable to shed their presence within me, even as an adult. My fear of insanity was wholly groundless, and floated away forever as she spoke, leaving me as eminently sane or crazy as most folk are who have their eyes wide open in this world.

Psychiatrist

You poke and pry
and painfully
explain to me
the punchline
of my sick joke.

While gradually

I'm killing myself

laughing.

AQUITTAL

When my daughter was six months old, she loved to sit on the rug surrounded by a few objects, which I tried to make sure were changed each day. I would sit with her quietly in the afternoons, reading and occasionally watching her out of the corner of my eye. She would pick up an object, taste it, feel it with tongue and lips, smell it, pass it repeatedly from right to left hand, put it behind her back, find it again, and repeat the whole performance, meanwhile talking to herself with soft enquiring gurgles. Finally, she would hold it out to me, and I would take it and say, 'Block. It's a block.' — and hand it back to her. Now she had explored everything about this block, including its verbal symbol, which she had checked out with me. She put it away and went on to the next object, for the possibilities of blocks are rather limited.

The possibilities of sex are less limited, but when I consider how my daughter went about exploring her world, it helps me to understand how ordinary small children approach finding out about sex. To the growing toddler blocks and sex are of equal interest, and carry equal emotional weight. Both carry sensual and intellectual information to be processed in the child's brain. Sex only increases in emotional weight when the child, upon holding out her question to the adult, is met with either sudden evasion, or a concrete demonstration of what sex means in adult terms.

This is what must have happened to me as a small child. Along with everything else that called for my attention to be explored, objects, animals, people, places, there was sex, and it was no less, but no more fascinating than anything else in my world. As with the baby and the block, I first of all tested my own physical sensations, as all children do. Then, since it was not a concrete object, but a sensation, I looked for further information, not from left and right hand, but from mother and father, the most obvious sources of information available.

If the left hand gives too little and the right hand too much information, the nature of the object being explored cannot be discovered. Accurate information coming from both hands is needed. But the ability of my parents to convey that information to me in a balanced way was impaired. What's more, the actual information was distorted, for it was geared towards me as if I had been an adult, with

110

an adult's understanding. For a child it was simply inappropriate information. Having no words for it, I could not handle it like a small block, but rather moved within this threatening area which enclosed me.

It could not be put behind my back while other things were being explored, yet the absence of a thing teaches as much about it as its presence. Its importance was consistently magnified out of all proportion, because of my mother's evasion, and my father's preoccupation with it. As a small child, my mind could not contain this enormous secret message, but only what it must mean about me, whose body somehow did contain it.

The left hand, my mother, gave no information except fear. The right hand, my father, gave far too much information, overwhelmed me, confused me with its wealth of sensual information, till I remembered the message of the left hand, and putting the two together, knew that this thing, childish sexual pleasure, so natural to every baby touching itself before its attention passes on to other things, this thing, for which I had no name, was hugely terrifying and wicked. The thing was wicked, and not my father. And because I contained this wicked thing, this feeling that was a part of me, it must be me who was wicked.

I was not allowed to put down this thing which had become impossibly painful to hold. My wickedness was held up to me by my father, and defined by my mother, though neither of them understood what was happening inside me. The only way to handle this huge, hideous block of horror was to perform an almost impossible mental trick, to, as it were, place what was inside of me outside of me, as the baby places the block behind her back. But because I had to do this with what was a part of me, I had to split myself in two. I had to forget. I had to hide this event from consciousness with all its accompanying feelings, so that it would remain forever hidden from view. As far as awareness of sexuality went, the clock stopped for me at the age of six. I was not allowed to find out about sex at my own

childish pace. Natural feeling became a thing that was for-
bidden to me by one parent, and forced on me by the other,
and the moment this happened, all possibility of sexual
enjoyment came to an end, not only then, but far into the
future, far past the time when it should have been mine by
right of adult loving commitment.

Tree

This tree I hide behind
displays its weals
where I have peeled the bark
to find larvae.

They burrow deeper in the wood,
escape the air
they dare not breathe outside the bark.
They like it dark.

I hold me still
to sense them in my doubt —
love biting fear.

But have to stand inside myself and out,
wood can't feel care.

I came to Eve as the mother of a child who was troubled,
and for whom I was afraid. A great deal of care was taken by
the clinic to build up my trust in their ability to handle my
child's needs with understanding and skill, so that I could
release him to his own play therapist. I could then allow
myself to become slowly conscious that I was not only
anxious as a parent, but that the hurt I felt for my child
was an accurate reflection of the anxious hurt child I also
was inside.

By the time the day came when I was able to reveal what

had happened to me, I had developed a mental picture of myself which lasted throughout that day, and for a long time following. In my picture I stood as a small child with hands outstretched to Eve, showing her the deep wounds in my palms, which were encrusted with dried blood and pus. Because she did not recoil from this ugliness, I was able to show her other cuts, weals, bruises and grazes all over me, as trustingly as a child to its mother, confident that no matter what needs to be done in order to heal the wounds, and no matter how much that hurts, the mother feels only affection and the desire to make everything better.

I was very tempted in some ways to minimise what happened, and in other ways to exaggerate. This temptation was made still more difficult to control because the memory returned in such a distressing, disjointed way, with abrupt halts and sudden flows of words that left me choking and gasping, as if I had been half strangled all my life. I was filled with exactly the feelings I would have experienced upon trying to tell my mother at the time it actually happened. Split many ways, I wanted to be protected from Eve's horror, shock, anger, disgust, withdrawal. With another part of me, I wanted to protect Eve from the impact of what I was saying, to minimise. And yet I also wanted, silently cried out for her to protect me. I would have given anything in the world just to be taken in her arms and cuddled. I even drew nearer to her after a while, hoping that she would make it easier in this way for me to go on remembering.

Most extreme of all was the fear of her disbelief. On the child level, I was sure she would not be able to accept this torrential pain I was pouring out, any more than my mother could have, that she would downplay everything and accuse me of over-dramatising. On the adult level, her disbelief of the actual event I was remembering, in addition to my own wildly fluctuating self-doubt, self-belief, would have been a direct threat to my sanity. Justifiable disbelief would be more bearable, if only marginally, because I would know that I myself had brought this about, and to that extent was in control of the rejection and confusion that her disbelief in the simple truth would have caused in me. For this reason, I had to test the ground, to take a false step forward as it were, by earning her disbelief, by in fact exaggerating what had happened.

The accusation never came, I did not have to defend myself in any way. On the contrary, Eve told me that she had known almost from the start that something of the kind I had described had happened to me. She had known I was a victim of sexual abuse, and had waited for me to tell her freely, and of my own accord. I was stunned by this, and still cautious. But her following words were so reassuring, built such a matter-of-fact atmosphere of trust, that after a time, I was able to backtrack and correct what I had said to the exact truth, still in horrible fear, but remembering how many times, in the months of preparation leading up to this day, Eve had explained in relation to other points of discussion, that she could only work with the material she was given.

Now the bare truth was out. I knew how much help I needed, and that no amount of sympathy would be worth the lost opportunity of that help, tailored to the precise injury I had sustained. Yet there had been so much ambiguity and pretence in my life, so much need to find protection for myself and give protection to my mother, so many hidden, conflicting feelings about both these huge needs, that to achieve at last, through enormous strain, a balance of reality on this one day, made it at once the most difficult day of my life, and the one with the most enduring effects. At the end of it, I knew there was nothing I could say, no matter how horrendous, wicked, ludicrous or trivial I thought it, that would damn or belittle me in Eve's eyes. Her reaction dealt with each separate splinter of fear at one stroke. She would never accuse me of lying, of making a fuss about nothing. I had been accusing myself of this all my life, partly because I knew my mother, in an attempt to deal

114

with the devastation of her world, would have done just this, and partly because there was indeed 'nothing' to make a fuss about – the 'nothing', the gap in my memory, in which I had been forced as a child to conceal my father's advances, in order to survive the horror of their occurrence.

There were many times, upon leaving Eve, that I wanted to thank her, and didn't, feeling the hopeless inadequacy of the commonplace words, how little they could possibly express what I wanted them to. But on this occasion I did thank her, struggling to convey to her the most important way of all that she had helped me that day. While encompassing me with her own personal security, her lack of fear, her trust in me, her gentleness and respect, she had not embraced me. She had not so much as held my hand or touched my shoulder, even at my mute request. What this cost her personally I do not know. Her compassion filled the room, surrounded the intensity of my agony, but did not touch it. I was left physically alone to feel the experience, to remember, comprehend and contain it, without distraction, on every level of my being. I was allowed space to receive myself back.

Now I knew what I was striving with, had always been striving with, to exhaustion. Now I had the measure of it, understood what it was I was sitting in this room for. Aware how seriously Eve was taking what had happened, I could afford to take it seriously myself, as I had never been permitted to do. I didn't know what, if anything, was going to happen next. I had no idea how much work was still to be done, but only that whatever this meant, I would attempt it, for in the end I was accountable not to Eve, but only to myself for my own well-being.

Upon my thanking her for not holding me, for respecting my primary need, she smiled, saying I didn't really want her to mother me, did I? I badly wanted to continue telling the truth, but I was silent, for there is no word in the English language that means both no and yes.

115

Quarry Woman

I came across you, damaged,
blasted from the land
that used to lock your secret fossils
into the rocks. There, where man
had used you and abandoned you,
they lay exposed, found out,
and you, flesh wounded,
torn from farm ground.

You hold your jagged arms
up to the sky, cracked woman,
the stone bowl holds water.
You accept what the sky sends, rain,
that you may reflect the sky
under the level of the ground.

It always seems to me, looking back, that the crucial instant
of the beginning of my healing came immediately after I
had told Eve about being sexually abused by my father. And
it came not merely because she had been able to accept and
comfort me, to tell me that what had been done had been
done to me, and not by me, but also because by waiting and
working for months to arouse the child within me to speak
and hear, and by using that time to build up my self-esteem
as a responsible adult, she enabled me to tell myself, and to
believe what I myself was saying. In asking me the question,
'What is child sexual abuse?' repeatedly, she forced me
to answer it eventually. The answer came from me, and
not from her to me. From my own lips, I heard what I
knew, but had not been letting myself know that I knew.
I did not trust myself, and Eve was more concerned
that I trust myself on this score, than that I trust her.
I had been so humiliated in childhood, that my trust not
only in others, but more essentially in myself, had been

completely destroyed. In confirming my own perception, not hers, Eve began to restore that self-trust, in the most fruitful moment, the moment of my relating the memory of the humiliation. In being able to reassure myself, rather than being reassured by her, I used my own maturity, and was able to see that my father had not used his, though he had used the power of it. I stopped looking up at him in my mind, as a frightened child would. Instead I was able to look across at him, adult to adult, and know that he had been in the wrong, not me. All this happened within a few minutes, thirty years later. Yet all the implications of those few minutes were so full of significance that it was enormously difficult for me to take in more than sounds of words, both mine and Eve's. The child inside me was instantly reassured. But the other layers of meaning took a long time to penetrate my comprehension.

Eve had to cover every eventuality. Neither of us knew what more there was to remember. It might have been that, having started the train of memory, I would continue, perhaps at a time when I was alone, finding myself again on the brink of a precipice of fear. So, very gently and with infinite respect, she suggested that it was possible that I had enjoyed what had happened with my father. My voice rose to a high and tiny pitch as I turned away, begging her not to say that. But she continued, steadily, calmly, explaining how it was possible for sexual abuse to be tender, for it to happen under the guise of affection, so that the child comes to believe it is in fact affection, and can be morally blackmailed into silence. I found it excruciatingly painful to contemplate, much less recall. If it did happen that way, it remained lost to my consciousness. Eve did not pursue it, allowing time to do any work that was necessary. If it was not there to be dealt with, no harm was done. I was not being accused, doubted, forced to confess. If it was there, her words would penetrate to where it was hurting and be absorbed, just as an injection of penicillin to a physical injury.

117

Meanwhile in order to divert her, as I thought, and also because I wanted to know, I asked her how it would be possible for me to have enjoyed being sexually abused. And Eve explained how it is not only perfectly possible, but normal, for children to be sexually aroused, even while watching television, though it does not have the meaning for them that it does for an adult, because it is merely a sensation for them, and forms no part of a relationship, even an imaginary one. This happens, she went on, with all children at some point, so casually that they hardly notice. If it had happened with my father, such stimulation would have been premature in that it did not arise naturally within me. But it would not have been the sexual arousal itself that would have harmed me. What did harm me, whether or not I was aroused, was the use of coercion, either in the form of physical violence or moral blackmail, the knowledge that what was happening was taking place because I was too young, weak and afraid to stop it, and all the power and authority, physical, social, emotional and intellectual, was on my father's side. My enjoyment perhaps even participation, would have been part of his ingenious way of ensuring that he would never be found out, that he never even had to face his own guilt. That I might feel guilty would not cross his mind, for I was not a person to him, but a kind of soft toy.

In this way, by giving me straightforward information, Eve helped me to recover from the pain of this fresh consideration, to think in relative calmness about the unthinkable. And I could feel her taking the weight of the burden of heartache I had held to myself for so long, even unacknowledged. After many months, she asked me about it in passing again, and I was still unable to remember anything except fear and shame, but could tell her this peacefully, without the utter petrification of horror I had at first felt. I knew it might still be there, lurking in my mind's shadows, but I had come to terms with it, feeling that any pleasure I might have experienced had been paid for a thousandfold by my inability to recognise it for the rest of my life.

Site

I sift the stones
to find the space between,
then sift the space
to separate the known.

What do I seek?
I seek what has been shown,
felt at my memory's first touch
of hand to hand,
stone to stone.

Stones turn to sand.
Still I work on alone,
sifting the dust of stones, hands, time,
as if I daren't not,
as if I must.

Eve was very emphatically not my mother, and the adult part of me would have resented deeply her trying to mother me, myself the mother of three children. Yet the picture of me going to her as a small maimed child, whose wounds were in sore need of attention, persisted, and was essential to me at this time, since the pain of her cleaning out those wounds, exposing each and every one to the healing fresh air, was very great. To do this, she not only asked me to tell her where it hurt, but when I'd finished telling her all I could, she indicated by suggestion that there might be more than I had told her, not doubting what I had said, but by telling me what sometimes happens with other survivors, in such a way that I was free to confirm some of these suggestions and deny others, according to the truth of my own experience.

First of all she drew on paper a diagram of my family, squares for boys, circles for girls, starting with the eldest, and finishing with the youngest, myself. Looking at it, talking about it with Eve, felt very strange, as if I was being drawn out of a dream, the events of which were being tabulated statistically.

Flickering from dream to diagram, I watched her put in symbols for my mother and father, draw lines from them to me. As youngest, she said, the abuse would be particularly damaging. I held on to this, uncomprehending, watching her thicken, with tiny frenetic zig-zag strokes, the line from myself to my father, while that between my mother and myself was comparatively faint. How did she know this? And what did it mean? I felt the tie between my mother and myself to be very strong indeed, too strong between mother and long-since-married daughter. I could not get free. As for my father, she seemed to be illustrating that the connection between us was charged with a taut emotion that was even fiercer than the dread, hatred and loathing I had just expressed for him. I kept these doubts to myself, afraid of their implications, of her answers if I should protest, waiting for further interpretation. It was too much for me to take in, I was still too deep in the dream from which Eve was beginning, but only just beginning, to waken me.

With the diagram between us, mapping out my position in the family, Eve went on to tell me, to map out for me, my position as a survivor in the world. I had always felt a one-off freak, even though I had only been semi-aware that this image of myself was a constant reinforcement of the state my father's abuse had left me in. Now it turned out I was not so different after all. Sexual abuse is extremely common, Eve said, spread widely through every strata of society. I took in every word hungrily, took them all home to savour, to digest, to feel their effects as they seeped through my being, illuminating all the pain of my past, the pain of being different, not quite part of the human species. Her words brought relief of not being a stranger everywhere on earth, an alien in clever disguise. They also brought fresh pain, as I realised there must be thousands and thousands still hiding in this hell of loneliness, not feeling themselves to be truly a part of humanity, watching others living, and not knowing how it is done naturally, without all the artificial aids a survivor needs in order to keep going.

Eve made it clear to me that I was very far from being alone. We discussed also the fact that some survivors are assaulted by other members of the family, uncles, brothers, grandfathers, by female relatives, by trusted adult friends, teachers, sometimes by the very people they turn to for help. She waited while I took this in, and something in her manner of speaking and waiting conveyed that if any of this had also occurred to me, it would be all right to tell her. None of this came as a memory. None of this happened to me. But she made me aware that whether the abuse had occurred frequently, with actual penetration and over a long period of time, or whether it happened just once, without penetration, with one trusted adult, it was still sexual abuse and seriously damaging. I need not be afraid of having suffered either too much or too little to receive her help. And she told me that she could help me, and had helped another survivor. This gave me the enormous reassurance of being in experienced hands. But, because she had specified 'another survivor', it did not make me feel I was on some sort of conveyor belt of survivors, all to be processed in the same way. I was not different, but I was individual.

Father's Child

Nowhere to hide
on the trim mown lawn
kept cropped by him
to keep it growing green.

121

Unseen
the child lies curled
on her side
in the wild grasses
waiting for moonless night
to womb her small, uncovered
embryo form.

Unremembered,
undiscovered,
her love,
kept cropped,
keeps growing green for him
to walk upon.

Only much later, pondering the memory of that diagram, I understood that it was not an illustration of how I saw things now, but of how they had been for me at the age of six. My mother had been a depressed, ineffectual shadow figure, impossible to arouse, even by my passionate need and mute appeals to her, always hanging around her, trying to get near her, touch her, receive her caress. My father was the important person around the house. I waited for his return in the hall every day, running to greet him at the door with a shining face of welcome, quickly, so he wouldn't even have to turn the key in the lock. But behind that memory there is another, that of calculating with anxious, six-year-old logic that this would please him, would maybe put him in a good mood.

I had to please him, to make him pleased with me. I had to escape the violence, the unexpectedness of his inexplicable wrath. Everyone else in the family seemed to suffer it, seemed to manage. I had only found one way to cope, to act as if I loved him, to act so well that I didn't actually know whether I did or not, and didn't ever dare to think it out.

This was the explanation of the thick, zig-zag line between

us. It represented the unspoken understanding between his canny old brown eyes, smiling at me quizzically from beneath his bushy eyebrows, and my large, blue, trying-to-be-innocent eyes. Always unsure whether or not he had seen through my act, unsure whether or not it was in truth an act, unsure of myself, of him, of everyone and everything, except that we were in something private, secret, together, and that I, alone of all the others, sometimes had this paradoxical way available to me to escape Daddy by letting him catch me.

I had to make myself believe my own act, or I couldn't have escaped, but would have known myself to be in a trap, and would have had no other way to escape that knowledge but to form some other story for myself, a story that would emerge as insanity. But it is all right for little girls to love their daddies. And so I adored my father, idolising him in the true sense of the word, He was not a person, but a god to be appeased, to be sacrificed to, to be feared and worshipped, simply by right of being my father, the father of my family. Everyone seemed to go along with this, including my mother. These assumptions seemed as solid and immutable as the huge grey stone bricks that made up the walls of our house. But not to Eve.

Each time I went to see her, I discovered that these assumptions that had walled me in could be challenged. They were challenged simply by being named by Eve, stated out loud. If she was right, I would tentatively confirm what she said, then go home and think about it, reassess it with adult judgement. Was it really true that success was to reach the very top of the tree, to be rich, famous, influential? Was it true that my parents' values were necessarily the best, split as they were between hidden and spoken values, both almost impossible to live up to? Was it true that I was just a vulnerable little girl, disguised as a woman? And if none of these things were true, then what was? What was success, what were my own values, how was I to view men, cope with them, what was it to become, to be, a woman?

The wall of assumptions, of expectations so sky-high that I hadn't been able to see over them began to crumble away. Each week I would come to Eve full of questions, to which there never seemed to be any pat answers. But nonetheless, I left her with my head full of new thoughts, which through the following week turned into even more questions. I myself began to take over the challenging process, searched for my own truths, and found in that search that I had a self to be true to.

Little by little, I discovered that I had formed a set of perfectly reasonable values of my own, conflicting with those of my family, and therefore never wholly relied upon, but definitely present. I began to explore them, test them, voice them. We talked about success, what I wanted from my life, the fact that I could have anything within reason, what 'within reason' would mean, what was realistic to expect, the difference between a dream, a hope, a plan. I came to see that I was by no means a failure, and, despite the dismal grind of my schooldays, by no means stupid. Unharnessed from self-doubt, I was encouraged to use my full intelligence, to assess and use what talent I had. I found I had no more to be ashamed about than anyone else. And all the blocks to my understanding of this simply melted away as I came to look at them from this new angle of being adult, more and more fully adult as I emerged from the confusing dream of my childhood. The door of the big grey house creaked open, and I came out, blinking in astonishment, into the real, wide-awake world.

Rat Nightmare

My voice in the dark
high and trembling
my mind running up and down
in the blue room.

124

(bundles of old rags
butt food scraps
crammed high beside the bin

she stands, hands on hips,
her eyes say
'squeeze them in the bin
and ram the lid shut.'

I freeze
between the bin
and the batches of crap

skin prickling to the rat
not really dead, nor ending,
but watchful at my back

fantasising the shred of my flesh
between its claws
the crack of yellow jaws
on my pinkness

she says 'it's dead'
but it's only pretending)

My voice in his arms
high and trembling
my mind stops running in the blue room
and squats, pretending.

On one side of the tightrope there was abnormal prudery,
ludicrous, old-maidish sexual inhibition. On the other side,
sluttishness, promiscuity, prostitution. At the end of the
tightrope, there was old man Daddy, always lying in wait
for me, waiting to laugh derisively, dismissively, if I fell off
either side. Waiting for me to come to him.

It was a nightmare of course. I knew that it, he, wasn't
real. If I could just walk through the smiling phantom
I could get free, would be able to put him behind me,

disentangle myself from his memory, his influence, his long shadow. I just had to be brave about it, that was all. If I could be brave, get beyond him, I would find out the meaning of the word 'love'. But I could not be brave enough. I would approach him slowly, warily, bracing myself for one last dash that would take me right through him. In nightmares, I never made it. Death never actually occurs to the self in dreams, and I would not allow it to happen to me. I would awake, whimpering, sobbing, high-pitched in the terror-filled blackness, babbling my dream into the silent reaches of the cosmos that our bedroom had turned into. In the morning I was myself again, the efficient housewife. I never knew when long spates of these nightmares would begin, why there were sometimes months of nocturnal blankness in between. I would not let myself understand that in my nightmare I was more awake to the truth than I was during the day.

The fear of men. Always afraid of rape. To see rape in the eyes of perfectly nice men whose only crime was that they were attracted to me. I was unsure, uncomfortable on the most innocuous social occasion, untrusting of men, and of myself. My husband rescued me from this dilemma. He offered relative safety. Marriage was a partial protection in a world of predatory men, to whom I was vulnerable. My marriage held them at bay, and within it, I held my husband at bay. Meanwhile, semi-secure in this protective custody, I stood as still as I could on the tightrope. Sometimes I wobbled a bit. Meeting a man at a party who flirted with me, made a pass, a suggestive remark, I became clumsy on my tightrope, On each occasion I came away helplessly angry at myself, at him. Again I had been inadequate, inept, squeamish, humiliated. Or, if I had leaned towards him too far, I was indeed the slut that I knew myself basically to be, dirty, worthless, humiliated in a different way. There was nothing I could do about these baffling, shaming situations. They were part of the nightmare, though I was wide awake.

Fantasy was the trance state that came half-way between

waking and sleeping. In fantasy, too, I had to cope with the phantom, to pass though fear, if I wanted to find, to make love. Making love was not impossible for me, as it is for so many survivors. It was part of the way I could prove to myself that I was normal. That, for me, was its main function. In fantasy I was able to rush the phantom, to run right through it as a hang-glider rushes at the edge of a cliff to take off, glide, soar, forget the effort of courage needed at the start. And I did forget it, every time. To remember would have been to ask why, and I couldn't afford that question. But neither could I forget what happened when I came to land, hearing the harsh, racking sobs that came from my throat for long afterwards each time, so loud, so uncontrollable, so utterly broken-hearted. The child within me remembered.

And my own children knew. I would emerge from the bedroom in the morning sometimes, to discover a small body curled in blankets on the floor outside, fast asleep after an anxious night spent waiting, listening, ready to rush to my defence if necessary. I had to tell them at the clinic. Listening to my voice speaking the terrible words, I knew what this admission meant. It meant I was not, after all, normal. This was not right. Tears following self-abandonment were not unheard of, but the depth of bitter grief that I reached went beyond the norm that was so necessary to me. Eve listened quietly, attentive to all I was saying, and all I was not saying. The children would be taken care of. And, in time, so would the child within me.

Leaf Lesson, Man Lesson

Now girls,
pick yourselves a leaf
from the privet hedge.
Run your finger round its edge,

examine it,
above
and beneath.
Bold young green and glossy ones
spring, this spring,
when you bend them.
And if you have picked
an old, thick,
moss-coloured one,
crack it in your fingers quickly.
A most satisfactory way
to end them.

Eve could not deal directly with my nightmares, though as a result of both our efforts, they did gradually cease. She could reassure me about what was normal, and how normal I was. Apparently fantasising was very common, as was crying, to a certain extent. If either brought me great distress then I could get help, though not directly from her.

It was in the realm of the uncertainties of everyday waking life that Eve could be a source of straightforward guidance. But I had to ask for that advice, which was not easy always, and particularly with regard to the social skills and savoir-faire with which, as a mature woman, I was supposed to be adequately equipped. I was learning, however, that if I really wanted something, I had to find a way of asking, and if it was sufficiently important, I did ask. As time went on, Eve would not let me ask in the round-about way I was used to, fearful of rejection or ridicule, relying on others' ability to guess, and disappointed if they didn't. Once or twice she picked out what I was trying to ask, phrased it in a question and got me to repeat it, so that I became conscious of how afraid I had been of asking assertively for what I wanted or needed, even of knowing what I wanted or needed. And this was the very obstacle that lay at the heart of my difficulties with regard to men.

Once or twice, approached by a man, I had not succeeded in keeping my balance on the tightrope. Concerned not to appear uptight, prudish, to seem as self-assured as a woman of my age ought to be, I had found myself in too close for my own comfort and had experienced the paralysis of extreme panic, an inability either to help or hinder what happened. Aware that this inability had the appearance of an invitation, I was nonetheless incapable of running away, transfixed as a baby rabbit by a snake, or as a child by an incestuous adult. But in spite of these terrifying ego-shattering experiences, I wanted to know, to be friends with, to come to terms with men. I wanted not to feel such an ingénue, not to subtly convey my inner state, as I was sure I must do, despite knowing and using all the correct social gestures. I wanted to be in control, and saw no way that this would be possible. And in any case, as a respectable married woman, I felt I had no business to experience any of these problems. Yet half the human race was lost to me, through nothing but fear.

I listened and watched Eve carefully for clues as to how she felt about these things, but it took me many months to explain my own problem, and to ask her directly what to do about it. It was important to me to be sure that she saw me first as a woman, rather than a married woman, that she would not moralise, but leave me free to decide things for myself. It was also important that she would not take advantage of my awkwardness and shyness to talk down to me. When I was sure about these potential pitfalls to my dignity, I asked her about it outright, feeling like a school-girl with her first boyfriend, asking how far it was all right to go, nervous, embarrassed, but, not foreseeing another opportunity, determined to find out.

The hardest part of the conversation came right at the beginning, when Eve asked me about Tim. I had complained about my difficulties with Tim, a would-be 'father-confessor' type friend, the trouble I had keeping him at comfortable arm's length, neither slapping him down, nor encouraging him too much. I knew he was attracted to me, and the subtlety of his approach scared and fascinated me. He was an interesting man, and we had a fair amount in common. The group in whose company we met prevented the intimate look in his eyes from being openly expressed, and I would have despised myself for withdrawing from such a harmless and otherwise happy relationship. Indeed I intended to use this example, which was not the first of its kind, to work with Eve's help on the general problem of men, and so I kept it ticking over gently, while the prospect of eventually getting that help allowed me to put up with the tension involved. For I was sure that without help, and without running away, I would not manage to control the situation. Even as it was, I had to put on a hard, invulnerable act, which did not seem to fool Tim for a minute, and left me feeling untrue to myself. But the question Eve asked me and which took me an endless and agonising age to answer was whether I was sexually attracted to Tim?

Not only was this very thought deeply disturbing, but in fact I simply did not know very clearly what the truth was. His attraction posed such a threat to me, that I had been too busy warding him off in my mind to pay much attention to my own level of attraction. But now for the first time I realised that Tim appealed to me in quite a physical way, as well as being a very nice person. He was also disarmingly kind, and all these considerations went to the making of a highly charged situation, within which I moved, semi-conscious of vibrations only too obvious and amusing to the rest of the group, I suspected.

Much to my amazement, Eve seemed to be not too surprised when I finally came out with the answer that, yes, I was attracted to Tim. Now, she said, we had something definite to work with. I, on the contrary, felt very frightened. I could not imagine where this was going to lead. But Eve told me I had just made the biggest step in controlling the course of events. I knew whether I was attracted or not, knew how much I was attracted. I was in possession of myself, and therefore could not be possessed without my consent. Tim was not going to rape me. He might try and seduce me, but I was not a child. Armed with self-knowledge, I could make a choice to move towards Tim, to move away, or to keep things as they were, only this time in control of how things were, a control that proceeded from awareness of my own desires, and from my own decision about what I was going to do with those desires. I might decide to do nothing, in which case, if directly approached by Tim, I could tell him of my attraction and of the fact that I had decided to do nothing about it. I could then remain quite comfortably in Tim's company, even sit right next to him, knowing I had been straightforward with him. It was not being straightforward with myself that had caused the problem.

I was not a child. I could make a choice. I sat staring at Eve, almost stupified by the freedom she had just given me, alternately laughing and questioning her some more, to make sure that it was really true, that I was really getting it right. It seemed so simple. Not to keep secret how I felt from myself, from Tim, from anyone, filled me with incredulous astonishment and relief. It was not a crime to feel. It was not a crime to feel anything at all. It was not a crime not to feel attracted either, even to feel utter repulsion and loathing. I did not have to pretend either way. I did not have to please, appease or run away. I was not the child I had been. This was what it was to become, to be, a woman.

How, or if, I chose to convey my feeling was another question, but one that hardly mattered, compared to my own inner certainty of what it was. If I was certain enough, my decision about it would convey itself in my eyes, my gestures, my whole stance. I would rarely need to speak, but could, if necessary. I could cope with men, with women, with anyone. I could cope with myself, if I could just accept myself.

But whatever I decided, whether the outcome was happy or sad, because I had actively made that choice rather than passively allowing events to take their course, I was fully

131

responsible for the results of my own decisions. I could not complain that I had been used, nor hide behind my marriage. But on the other hand, if things went well I could legitimately pat myself on the back and take the credit. I could learn from my mistakes, claim and rejoice in my successes. I could take care of myself, take charge of my own life.

My head was buzzing with all these new possibilities. Like a newly uncaged bird, poised for flight, I was impatient to go and start living. I was also sad for the loss of so much time spent so worried and tense that I had been unable to relax in company, fighting and running, striving to polish my balancing act, to achieve calm, elegance, stability. I knew I had just received the good mothering I had needed twenty years before. I thought of my own daughter. When the time came, I had so much to give her, to pass on to her. She would not be handicapped as I had been. She would not need to defend herself so desperately against being used. She would be strong and brave and happy in her youth and beauty, as neither her mother nor her grandmother had known how to be.

Whore's Curse

You take my hand? Why?
Come, screw me,
there's no need to fake,
I understand.

What, you wish you knew me?
Would have me slowly,
take the grand tour?

Well then,
be sure you bear in mind beforehand
how I loan
the looks and tones of voice,
the time
between each cursed hook.

If you won't take me
up against a wall,
don't want to know
the kind of girl I am,
a call girl,
do not say inside yourself
'I do not have to pay.'

For it will cost you
more than all you own.
Those woman's needs you've known
and failed to feed
will soon have grown to one,
which I'll consume —
your very self.

It was my poetry that saved me. Otherwise I wouldn't
have known how to realise or express my deepest fear to
Eve. But the poetry which has been going on in my head
all my life had escaped on to paper sometimes, and one
day, while shuffling through some papers, I came across
the poem 'Whore's Curse'. I picked it up and read it
slowly, over and over, with absolute concentration. By
now, I was aware enough to realise that every poem was
written out of vital need, and that no word was wasted.
Looking at this one, I felt myself slipping again into the
'other place' in my mind, the place of anger, shame, distrust, self-hatred and revenge. I have always felt a strange
sympathy with whores. Their fabled hardness, I knew
instinctively, was a cover for an infinity of pain. No
amount of money could ever make up for the living death
of a prostitute's existence.

But how *could* I know this 'instinctively'? I remembered
all the films I'd seen, operas, books, documentaries, paintings,

featuring in some way a prostitute. Each engaging my special attention, moving me, so that, for a while after absorbing each insight into the inner lives of prostitutes, I would be strangely disturbed and tearful. Was it sympathy, or was it affinity?

I sat down in a chair with my poem, gazing at its hurt, hurtful words. They were addressed to a man, a man who loved me. They were my words. I held on to the piece of paper, trembling violently. To stop myself shivering I crossed my arms, pressing the poem to my breast, and hugged myself, moaning and rocking, my tears falling on to the paper drop by drop. I knew about prostitutes because I was one. I simply could not remember a time when I had not known that.

It didn't matter that I did not actually practise my trade, that I had kept up a fine show of respectability, that I had never had a single extra-marital affair, that I didn't even have the courage to flirt with a man. I knew, and had always, always known that my husband had rescued me from a life of prostitution. The words written on the paper told me that, placed my deepest fear outside of me physically, on to paper, where it would wait until conditions were right for me to see and understand it.

I was alone with it, and had always been alone with it. And yet, I do not believe it was by any accident that I was searching through that sheaf of poems on that particular day. The secret part of my mind remembered writing the poem, and led me to search for it. For it understood itself not to be alone now. I would be seeing Eve the next day.

Not knowing how else to approach it, for it seemed such a fantastic proposition, I simply told her about the poem and how it had affected me. It was like giving birth to some misshapen monster. When it came to using the word 'whore' or 'prostitute', I could not bring myself to do it. It seemed I was trying to express adult concepts in a child's language of feeling. At the age of six, I hadn't known what a

134

whore was, only that a whore was a bad girl, sexually bad, therefore was what I was. Trying to reconcile the two languages, the two viewpoints that my head contained, I finally came out with, 'I think, I mean, I must think, I am a . . . tramp.'

Eve could have explained why I thought that, could have analysed the damage done by incest, traced my fear to its source. Had she done so, I would have been satisfied on an intellectual level, surprised, perhaps fascinated, and totally unchanged emotionally. In the event, she told me that she knew I'd had that fear, and had been going to bring it up sooner or later anyway. She asked me if I had in fact ever been a tramp, and I thought back through the years. 'No', I found myself saying, slowly and thoughtfully. 'Well, if you haven't been a tramp up till today, you're not likely to start being one now, are you?'

That was all she had to say. Like a deft midwife, she caught the monster as it was born and held it up to me. Her words were common sense. Anyone could have said them, and I would have been forced to agree, but the child inside me would not have been convinced. When Eve spoke, the whole of me heard, not just the adult part. She did not exploit me, abuse my trust with this power. She used it to help me become more powerful. She was like the good fairy godmother in the story, who had not been able to unwish the bad spell, but was able to put a time limit on its effectiveness, so that I could wake up eventually and not die. It was part of the long dream of all my years that I was a whore. With the simplest of words, in the twinkling of an eye, Eve was able to show me that it had only been a bad dream, a dream that was never going to come true.

In my eyes, she took on the role of loving mother. As I had once been towards my own mother, I was as openly receptive to her as a child. Knowing this, but consistently and continuously affirming my own authority in the situation, as well as hers, she used the enormous powerhouse of my emotion towards her as a learning room, a room where she untaught untruths, until the truth stood self-evident, and I could declare myself not guilty and go free. By not being afraid to take and use the power of my love for her, she enabled me gradually to claim for myself with confidence the dignity that is the rightful inheritance of every human being.

RECOVERY

It was not that he didn't love me. I knew he loved me. I only had to glance up at the subtle pastel drawing he had made of me, which hung in the corner of the living room so eloquently, to know exactly how much and why my husband loved me, to know just what it was he saw as he worked at it with the truthful hands and eyes of love. I was so moved by that drawing, not because he had portrayed me as beautiful, but because the beauty that was there was descriptive of the quality of his yearning and mine blended together. The brow and eyes were troubled and full of inescapable pain. The gaze was level, deep, strong. The hair was a veil of sorrow. In the act of making the drawing, he was reminding me, was reminding himself, that under and behind all the problems we had in speaking to each other, there was a constant, wordless continuation of a loving conversation which had begun at our first meeting, even the faint memory of which gave hope of somehow getting back there to that place where the conversation had begun to drift, stumble, threaten and fall silent.

It was not that he didn't love me. It was that I didn't love me. It was that I had accepted all my life that they were right. I could not be loved, I was not worthy of being loved. I was everything my parents had shown me to be, and this made me by definition unlovable. And I believed this so firmly, so implicitly, so unquestioningly, that it was as much a part of me as my bloodstream and circulated in my being in much the same way. I could not accept his love, could not believe it, and yet demanded it, unable to appreciate, add to, return or simply enjoy it.

And so at last, his love repeatedly rejected, he began to accept my version of me, to act, in sheer self-defence, as if he too shared my vision. And for that I could not forgive him. Everything turned bitter with such slow, imperceptible, subtle poison that somehow neither of us were ever able to face up to the fact that our marriage was almost dead. Behind the image of young lovers running hand in hand through fragrant cornfields lay other, more sinister and frightening images, which could not be talked about, and behind which lay the consciousness, in both of us, of disappointment, apprehension, time passing, a promise too long unfulfilled.

We were sitting together beneath the portrait of me, freshly drawn, when Eve finally managed to get us to admit to all this. When it came right down to it, I did not find it too difficult. Giving up the 'young lovers' illusion was easy when I knew I was not going to be left emotionally alone, for I had Eve. I really did not see why there was all this fuss, all this insistence that each of us, one after the other, should say, and hear the other say, that our marriage was a farce.

It did not worry me, partly because I relied on what I saw of our underlying love in the portrait to pull us through, as I always had. But mostly because Eve's very presence in our lives gave me the confidence that in some way that I did not know, but felt very sure of, everything would come all right.

It was very late. Eve should have left a long time before. She was speaking about something new now. She was telling us that she was leaving. She was not leaving our house. She was leaving our lives. She was taking an opportunity that had unexpectedly come her way to take a job she had always wanted, working with hurt children. I couldn't hear the words clearly. Couldn't believe those that I was hearing. Silence fell. I became aware of it, aware also of the fact that they were both looking at me, that I was supposed to say something, to respond.

I wanted to respond, to pass it off somehow, to get through some time until I could be alone. I could not feel. The pain was so enormous that my mind had gone numb, in self-defence. More words were being said now, some of them by me. I didn't know what they were, except that they were foolish. 'Two months' came through. I had two more months. That was something to hang on to. I didn't dare think beyond that. Aimlessly, I asked her if she liked the new portrait. She looked at it, said yes, she did, but she wanted to see me looking happier. The final irony, I thought, when I had only just died.

I put together everything that happened that evening, the situation of our marriage laid bare, Eve's withdrawal from that situation, having to collect our children from where they were being looked after, feed them, put little Frances to bed, pass time with the other two somehow until their bedtime, our separate silences as we lay together that night. Slowly, over the next few days, as the grief grew shockingly real and heavy, it came to me that appalling though her loss was going to be, this grief was not only about that. This loss was merely the echo of so many other losses, that the full realisation was almost impossible to take on board at all.

I had lost a beloved brother to his inner world, and a beloved sister to the world outside my family. I had lost my father, first, because he abdicated fatherhood, and then, because he had died behind my back. I had lost my innocence, my right to a carefree childhood, my femininity. I had not only lost, but never really had, my mother, and now, I was going to lose Eve. Each morning, as I woke up and remembered, my eyelids seemed heavier and heavier to lift. I did not want to see.

And yet also in the memory of what happened that evening appear the seeds of everything that went toward the recovery of all those losses.

First, the impending loss of Eve gave me the raw consciousness of what those losses must have meant to me, a harsh gift, but precious, because true.

Second, though we were unable to speak aloud, almost drowning in the fear of what we ourselves had said about our marriage, my husband still managed to speak in the most powerful way he could at the time, and on the same wordless level, I heard him. He took down the portrait from the wall, and spent the rest of the evening remounting and reframing it, so that it spoke out more boldly than ever, emphasising not what we had lost, but what we really had. Nothing was said, and yet everything was said, everything that essentially mattered. I was not comforted that night, for wordless communication was not enough, had not been enough for too long. We had to learn how to speak aloud, and without Eve's insistence, we would never have known how badly we needed that learning.

Third, there is the memory of the children, of their feeding, of their care, of their sleeping, of their total innocence, unknowing of the events of that evening, knowing only that I was full of tears. I had the children. I had the power to make their lives sing, or to make them search eternally as I had, for something unknown, lost, unrecognisable. I knew this power, had felt it from the first moment of my first pregnancy, had felt the awesome responsibility, the anxiety of not being able to fulfil that responsibility. Looking at them as they watched television that evening, while my husband cut card and made framing on the floor, I weighed up the losses against the gains, against what I actually had in my hands at that moment. I had two more months with Eve. I would use them. I would do whatever I could, whatever was necessary. I had lost enough, and would not throw away what was left.

Winter came, and with it, barrenness. Eve was lost in the city somewhere. She had appeared from nowhere, from among a thousand thousand faces, had brought me to life, to know what feeling meant, and then had disappeared, leaving me to feel, to feel her loss, day and night, forever. Even before she had said goodbye, she left again and again in my dreams, smiling, retreating, smiling. Reassuring me of my ability, but constantly going, with me half-believing her, until it was too late, and she was gone.

I ought to feel angry. She had said I ought to feel angry. But she had done nothing wrong. It was just unfortunate. There was no one to blame, least of all her, for whom I felt nothing but love, gratitude, sorrow.

Each morning I took Frances to nursery, almost dumb, thankful that for another morning Frances would be spared the silence of my misery. Returning home, the pain was tangible, red bloody meat slowly, perpetually being ripped apart inside my chest somewhere. So relieved to have three hours when I need make no effort to pretend it was not so. Moving around the house mechanically, hoovering, washing up, cleaning, tidying away a thousand pin-sized objects to their proper places, sometimes I would stop, transfixed by the image of her doing the same. She too must hoover, must peel potatoes, must rub stains from carpets. I had never of course seen her doing these things in real life, and so to have such a picture so clearly imprinted in my mind meant that I had stolen a bit of her to keep. I knew her, was watching when she didn't know it, and was briefly comforted. What this meant I had no idea, and was therefore afraid of. There were people to meet and talk with, tasks to be done, hours, days, weeks, years to pass somehow. Always, even with only a minute to spare between distractions, my thoughts returned to her like homing pigeons. Sometimes I wondered if she knew it. If the sheer power of my yearning would some day bring her to my door. But it never did.

I got so weary. She had left me her phone number at work, but I didn't use it. That might only make things worse. Besides, I knew she was very busy, and what could I say? There was nothing I could say that made any sense.

140

There was no name, no limit for this foolish, bewildering, shameful grief. There was no one to share it with. I did not want to lay it on my husband. We had too much else to sort out between us. I spoke to him of her only as a last resort, when sorrow overwhelmed shame. He was kind and gentle with me, patient in his own suffering.

Sometimes it helped to know that it was precisely because of the way I had felt about her that she had been able to help me so much. That this distress was the price of clarity. Sometimes that very thought made it hurt more than ever. It had all been planned, I had been tricked into feeling, used once again. But this time, used for my own good, not played with. And so reason and pain formed a tight head-band that circled my mind, chasing each other round and round until my head was dizzy and ached with the sharp thorns of thought.

There seemed no way to contain it, no end to it, no limit to its scope, no way to tell if it would get better or worse. One day I heard on the radio a voice describing the death of a loved one, and siezed on what was being said. This was the way to limit it, the way to name it. It was not an isolated phenomenon, known only to me. Its name was bereavement. It had been studied, charted. Others had been here before. There were even books written about it, new insights into it. I read them carefully, searching for an outer time limit. Six months? A year? Two years? Apparently, despite their similarity, bereavement was not like cancer, the tumour did not grow but diminished. One day I would not feel like this. How it would come about I could not imagine.

Meanwhile we had started work on our marriage, meeting with two counsellors, exploring without touching, circling each other warily, occasionally stumbling into each other's arms almost by accident. The sessions were never easy, never relieving or comforting in the slightest. I felt continually threatened, accused, called to account. I was being challenged, sounded in a new and unfamiliar way, and by a man and woman together. We, too, challenged them. We were not easy to help, though we were both striving mightily. Tense though the sessions were, they were nothing to the tensions we experienced at home, without the help of mediators. This was the only distraction from Eve that I willingly engaged in. It seemed the only hope of a new kind of way to be. And slowly it began to work, began to take over. We would look at each other in surprise, after a gruelling three hour session of thrashing through some problem, not hiding hurt, but not overpowered by it. Success was the achievement of a solution without dishonesty, trickery, fury, withdrawal. Our successes grew more and more frequent. New issues kept appearing, kept being dealt with. We were left more and more on our own as we became able to cope. My father was not touched upon, though they knew about him. He had struck us dumb from the grave. We were dumb with fear, even in the midst of our rage and disappointment. But we were given back our voices, and taught how to use them gently and precisely, to heal many wounds.

Spring passed, and summer. I had met Eve in the spring a year before, and each new kind of flower opening was a fresh reminder of her loss, a reminder which closed off any other kind of emotional possibility. Solving problems, though satisfying, did not stir the heart. Still, confidence was growing. We were not going to break up. We seemed to be succeeding as adults, as parents, as reasonable people.

Autumn ripened, fruit hung heavy on branches, seeds blew away. How does feeling begin? It begins in the primitive child within each of us, who plays in the silence of night. In the clasp of hands seeking the texture of skin, seeking to fill the emptiness yawning between human hearts, seeking for a common aim that has nothing to do with reason, but everything to do with hunger, hunger for a passion that extinguishes the light of reason. One day there was no feeling of love, only its knowledge, its manifestation in difficult striving. The next day, and from then on, the knowledge of feeling, of sexual delight, was present to me as a great revelation.

That first morning, looking at my face in the glass, touching it with wondering fingertips, I knew my body as a new thing. People were in the streets, walking about with pre-occupied expressions, people at business, in offices and shops, people who went home at night and drowned in this overwhelming whirlpool with their lovers. I wondered how they could keep the smiles from their faces, how such joy could be so concealed, could keep from spilling over into each minute of each day. Our honeymoon was beginning, after sixteen years of marriage and three children. And I looked again in the glass and knew it was possible to feel sky-great happiness, and for that happiness to be completely separate from Eve.

I should have guessed. Should have known the danger. I had let Eve invade my being, opened my spirit, allowed her to touch it with love, rendered myself liable to great injury and received it. Now he, too, could hurt me. We could hurt each other differently, more piercingly than ever before, because the contrast between acceptance and rejection, tenderness and withdrawal, was marked in an entirely new way, a way that involved the totality of our new-found intimacy.

And now at last I could be angry with Eve. I lay for hours, staring at the wall, fantasising her punishment for leaving me, figuring out where she was vulnerable, where I could possibly hurt her, if only in fantasy. I no longer cared whether or not she was to blame, whether or not this made any sense. Exhausted, I would fall asleep, to wake in the morning bewildered at the wasted hours, ready to try again to get back to reality.

After a while I came to realise that the image of Eve was intricately bound up with the child inside me, the child that had been, and still could be hurt by abandonment. If my

143

husband abandoned that child that he loved and played with at night, that child within me would seek for the mother, for Eve, and not finding her would mourn and rage, not in secret now, but openly, not needing any rational cause. This could be the only reason why the pain of her loss was only present now when my husband and I failed in communication, and cast back upon myself, I knew loneliness again. Therefore the way forward was clear. I knew what happiness was, knew that it was available to me, and mine to give, too. There were ways to arrange that it would be increasingly available, to permanently rid myself of the pain about Eve, to invest the present with enchantment.

In the daytime I grew up, exercised self-discipline, patience, foresight, as much wisdom as I could muster. At night I fell into tumbling childhood again. By both day and night trust grew, trust that I was never going to be permanently abandoned, a consciousness of being urgently needed and loved, a confidence that no row heralded a final disaster. Days flowed into nights that flooded the next day. No matter how busy we were, or what the problems, deep down we were calm and very sure about each other. Very little now could be badly wounding. Somehow, sometime, without even noticing I had done it, I let go of the safety-rope that was Eve.

I had no image of her to keep. No photograph, no tape of her voice. I knew I had let her fall away, that I could not carry her memory, not because it was too heavy, but because, beloved as it was, it was taking space, space that was needed for new loving. And so I made an image of her, as truthfully as I could, knowing that it was only an image, that I could never really know or own her, but only the portrait of her that I have drawn here with words, so that in releasing her likeness on to paper, I no longer need to bear it in mind, but nonetheless have it always in safe keeping, to look at with wonder and thankfulness for the recovery of so much that had been lost.

Buds

They opened in a dark room silently,
where I was watching,
secretly.

Now their bright blooms,
shatter the pastel patterns of my living room
with clarifying colour.

They will be dying soon,
like all else
forming part of the secret architecture
of a smile.

SURVIVING TOGETHER

For an Incest Survivor

There came a moment in that room
where I'd been listening,
where I'd been seeing you as not the same
as me, where I'd been hiding
from myself, and you, and all the rest,
where I'd been hearing how he murdered you,
and murdered you again,
and once again, and could not kill.

I will remember
for the moment still survives,
still holds the ache of love gone out to your despair.
There in the room
something in each of us began to live.

I drove home after my first incest survivors' group meeting, and sat for a long time in my car outside the house, trying to take in the vision I had seen for the first time that night, of the harm that incest does, the lives ruined, relationships unhappy, or broken, or impossible to undertake, survivors' children scarred, the loneliness, grief, guilt, the physical and psychological punishment meted out to victims for the rest of their lives. That I had suffered thus I knew, and had mostly come to terms with. That this same suffering had a thousand faces, a thousand variations, and yet that these variations were on the same themes, the same issues as my own, made me know that I was only beginning to see, that I had just caught my first glimpse of a boundless ocean of pain.

I was not at the group because I needed help. I was there because I felt I could give help. I didn't need help any more, I thought. I was the 'finished product'. But as we went round the group introducing ourselves, saying why we were there, it seemed that most of us were there to give help. We were all helpers, all prepared to bear each others' burdens. Perhaps bearing burdens was the only thing that we all felt qualified to do.

Hearing that many of us held the same aim as I did, made me wonder if, after all, I had come through the pain of incest. Perhaps I was fooling myself. At the time I was still mourning the loss of Eve, and that remained such a tender wound that I did not feel able to let anyone in that room touch it. Yet there was a need in me to express my loss somehow, though I didn't think that I was able to do it, that anyone in the world would be able to understand what I couldn't fully understand or accept within myself. It was this deep fear of unique pain, together with the inability to trust others enough to share it, that united me in spirit to the others in the group. Each of us carried many losses, sustained in many different ways. Our backgrounds, ages, educational levels, races, religious beliefs and sexual preferences varied widely, making it difficult for each of us to believe that we could all suffer in quite the same way our common tragedy. But just walking into the room that the rape crisis collective provided, into a group of incest survivors, for the first time, brought relief at the most basic level.

The simple sight of what looked a perfectly ordinary gathering of women, one that could have been picked at random from any city street, mirrored back to me, as nothing else could have, that incestuous experience had not put me at one remove from the rest of the human race. No one there was the freakish alien we had each, in our secret souls, conceived ourselves to be. This was the very first gift we gave to each other, just by sharing our physical presence.

We were there in safety, in the anonymity of first names only, to find a way to help ourselves and each other. To say where our pain was originally coming from was too difficult that first meeting, and indeed some never found the courage, or, perhaps, the need, to go into details of how they had been sexually abused. What came easier to most of us at first was to try to trace the more recent history of our search for meaning, for contact, and for healing. It was easier, but not easy.

I think of Cara, the only one of us with enough objective evidence and outside support to have been able to accuse her father in court. He had been convicted and sentenced to four years, commuted to two, for good behaviour. Two years imprisonment for seven years of incestuous abuse, starting when Cara was ten. While he was inside, Cara had had a few meaningless cosy chats with a social worker, a full year after the court case. That was all. Cara had, with huge effort, gained qualifications to get a job within those two years, so that she could be independent, and wouldn't have to be at home when he came out, untreated and unchanged.

I think of Pat, so young, and recently escaped from her violent stepfather, rehoused in a tiny flat perched in the top corner of a vast, bleak, multi-storey building, with dizzying balconies overlooking the sprawling acres of the city, though she was known to be suicidal.

I think of gentle Susan, whose voice was almost breaking as she told of the hospital where she had spent hours every day in a huge mixed patients therapy group of men and women, impassively expected to bare her soul in front of men who were quite unrestrained in their coarse comments about women, whose use of art therapy was brazenly pornographic.

I think of Joanne, standing in front of the Children's Panel at the age of fourteen, caught for persistent truanting and running away from home. Of her fine scorn for the gentleman behind the desk, who kept reproaching her for running away — 'when you come from such a good home.'

I think of Julie, who believed in being honest, and who tried with all her might to trust her psychiatrist, telling him that she had found some comfort in her father's caresses, that he had been the only one in her environment who had cared for her. I think of how this precious, most timid admission was used to hound her for months, to pressure her into confessing that she had deliberately set out to seduce her own father.

I think of Maria, whose sympathetic psychologist sits on the other side of a desk taking notes while Maria talks, how this has gone on for years without either of them realising the stalemate that the notebook, and the necessity for it, represents.

I think of Jean saying that she couldn't come back to the group, that she couldn't bear to fathom at last the full extent of everything that has happened to her, that she couldn't stand to hear the pain of her own life story echoed back to her in the words of the other survivors talking about theirs. Tragedy heaped upon tragedy over the years, leaving her alone and finally understanding the huge weight of retribution that has fallen upon her for having been a little girl who didn't know how to refuse her father. Jean, who has never had anyone to help her through, and who did come back nonetheless, sensing at last an opportunity to use the courage she has needed as a survivor to face what has happened to her, in the open.

I think and I think, and my brain seems to grow bigger than my skull can continue to contain. My thought seems to throb with the pitiless vastness of this new knowledge, and with the knowledge of pain I have not even been able to guess at, beyond the walls of the room where we meet, out into the streets, streaming into the thoughts of women who hurry past. One in ten. At the very least, one in ten have been sexually abused by a trusted adult. One in ten struggles alone with the lost ability ever to trust again. But when we do find ourselves being asked to trust again in 'someone who knows', someone we conceive to be 'up there' in a professional capacity, there can come again that disbelief, accusation, indifference, scorn, that further abuse of power, which has been invested in the name of healing, and which only reaffirms our lack of worth in our own eyes.

A few months before I had joined the incest survivors' group, I had received an invitation via the poetry circle to participate in the Women's Health Fair by reading my poems. In the privacy of the homes of fellow poets I had done this before, but I had never explained their context, had never made it quite clear what they were about. Now I wanted to tell. It wasn't enough to tell Eve, to repair the damage, to say goodbye to her, and then live on, with the whole cataclysmic experience of childhood and therapy swirling through my thoughts, but locked in for the rest of my life. I wanted to tell, but I didn't know who wanted to listen, if anyone. And here in my hand was a possible answer. An invitation to tell, an audience to tell.

I held the receiver to my ear, listening to the phone ringing at the other end and wondering nervously what I was going to say when it was lifted. The voice that answered was gently receptive, warm, thoughtful. I knew immediately that it was going to be all right, that, once again, I would be looked after while I told, and that what I told would be valued.

And so began a further extension of the journey I had believed had come to an end. I spoke to the women at the Health Fair. I told my pain and my poems. I felt the great wave of warmth flowing back to me. And I learned, too, how many women gathered at random in that room had suffered in a similar way, because then and there, they, too, told about it.

A whole new world of women who were concerned about incest was revealed to me, a movement among the womens' movement. I met women who had already started to tackle the problems of incest in our society, who had felt impelled to respond to the huge number of appeals for help from incest survivors which they were receiving, when ostensibly they were offering support only to rape victims. One third to one half of new phone calls to rape crisis centres are about incest, either happening currently, or, more often, in the past.

I found that, while I had been working with Eve, new initiatives had been afoot in my own city to try to begin to understand the situation of incest survivors, that a conference had been held. Incest survivors' groups had been started by Edinburgh and Glasgow Rape Crisis collectives, independent groups of survivors had gathered and begun to work on their problems in various parts of the country, the RSSPCC had started a group, and concerned women, survivors and non-survivors, had formed a country-wide association to act against incest and sexual abuse. It was thus that I came to know some of the strongest, and yet most gentle people I have ever encountered. I explored what groups were available, became a member of one, and began to face the darkness again, both on my own behalf and on others'. By now, that darkness for me was no longer a deep well out of which I didn't know how to climb. It was more like a night that I knew would, in time pass into day. But I could remember how it had been, and be there for the other women, at least a little as Eve had been there for me.

It took me a long time to understand some of what was happening in the group. Often, I would go home feeling very torn-up inside. At times I felt a oneness with individual survivors which went so deep that I felt almost as if I was them, although in every exterior way we were different. Perhaps these were moments of love. There would also be enormous rage on the others' behalf. We all experienced this. After a time it came to me that this seemingly passive activity of listening and absorbing, and the responses of pain and anger for another person, were familiar. The 'other person' was me. I felt within me something of what I had felt happening when I looked at and absorbed the words I had written down in the letters about my childhood. Previously we had allowed ourselves to feel for each other. That was all right. But for each of us, sooner or later, came the awareness that the anguish we felt for each other was also, and with increasing intensity as the realisation dawned, for ourselves.

We had feared and fought against self-pity, fended off the indulgence of pain, but the hard accepting silence which had become a lifetime's habit was undermined by others' tears, tears of sorrow, rage, loneliness, meaninglessness, tears which each survivor had held inside, unable to release in any other way. For each of us had taught ourselves with consummate skill not to feel, not to cry, not to know about the great reservoir of grief within us. More than anything we had been afraid of losing the innermost grip on our control, of 'letting ourselves down', of being swept away in the deluge of our own tears. But owning what belonged to us, with support, brought some measure of control, and this increased as we explored the extent of our anguish, and discovered at last that it was finite, and that we had survived, and could now go on to live.

Not all incest survivors' groups attempt to work so

deeply. Only those with strong, loving, experienced leaders can bear to accompany survivors in their depths, to share the utmost bereavement that incest is. True self-help groups, with no non-survivors or acknowledged leaders, can alleviate each others' loneliness, sympathise with each others' fears and offer support and encouragement in the many day-to-day living problems that result directly or indirectly from previous incestuous experience. But to open the inner wound to survivors who we know are as wounded as we are is to take a risk that not only will there be no one strong enough to contain and deal with our agony, but that we might cause further harm to our friends, since no one knows how much pain anyone, particularly a survivor, can take.

Those groups that have good leaders, whether professional or voluntary, permit complete release of feelings in utmost interior trust, and this kind of trust, born of a feeling of profound safety, is often our very first inkling that someone, somewhere in the world *can* be trusted, and that therefore the world might not be quite as menacing as we pictured it, and we ourselves might not be entirely at its mercy.

Another gift that non-survivors bring to the group is that, while understanding where our perceptions are coming from, they can put forward their own, which either validate ours, emphasising our commonly felt human feelings, or help us to see that we are perceiving life as more threatening than it really is. Meg, for instance, was afraid to walk in a certain notorious street, because she would be taken for a prostitute and picked up. The other survivors present when she said this could well understand and sympathise with this fear — but it took a non-survivor to point out that she would not be picked up, unless she gave her consent. She could, if she chose, refuse, walk on and survive the experience, without any dishonour. Indeed she had already survived a much worse experience, without any dishonour.

Some survivors hate the idea of groups, and would not find them helpful. Others can envisage being able to share their secret only in the presence of those who have been through the same experience. I needed to work individually and at great depth with someone whose personal approbation appeared to equal, and more than equal, that of my parents. Not everyone needs or can take such an intensity of relationship.

For all who work with survivors, whether it be individually or in groups, voluntarily or professionally, the qualities of stability and patience, emotional strength and sympathy are vital. But what will actually bring about our healing is the degree of acceptance and respect which can be offered to us, just as we are. How hard helpers have worked in the cultivation of these qualities within themselves, is manifest in their success in healing, or lack of it.

I remember Rose, who related her experience in hospital of finding a hidden tape recorder switched on behind a book on her therapist's desk. Her anger and sense of betrayal, her sweeping of everything on his desk on to the floor, brought punishment, and she was placed in a locked ward – 'for being unable to control herself'. And after my own fury at the stupidity of this cruelty had died down, I asked myself precisely what it was about this incident that initially harmed Rose. It was not the tape recorder, though the necessity for that remains a mystery. It was the fact of its being hidden, that the therapist did not have the courtesy that one human being owes another, to ask Rose's permission to be taped. It is this common courtesy, this inborn, instinctive respect, which restores to a broken person their sense of self-worth, self-respect. This therapist had overlooked the obvious. He was dealing with a fellow human being as worthy of respect as he was. He had within his grasp a remedy many times more powerful than all his drugs and tranquillisers. That he could not use it in the therapeutic situation spoke more of his faulty perception than hers. It was as much a faulty perception of himself as of Rose.

It is this perception of themselves that those who are really helping survivors are working on, by balancing the respect and acceptance that they extend to us with self-respect and self-acceptance. In this way, they do not ask anything of us that they have not asked themselves, previously and privately, about their own fears, angers, pain and guilt. To the extent that they are relaxed, we can eventually relax. Particularly with regard to their sexuality, successful helpers are free from needless worry and guilt, facing and accepting themselves through and through so that no survivor comes up against a barrier of fear, which reflects and confirms her own fear, wordlessly.

Coming to grips with incest opens in every human being areas of the self which are normally unquestioned. It is these unknown, unexamined parts of ourselves which are possible sources of fear. But the less the therapist fears, the more scope the survivor has to grow in while they work together. Therefore those who would heal survivors must be whole, or aware that they are not. It is unawareness and self-rejection that hurts, that makes the task personally painful, that slows down the work, and that cannot fail to damage further the frail self-esteem of an incest survivor.

As survivors and helpers we are equally preparing ourselves, taking it on as a lifelong task, which is the human task of knowing ourselves. To know all our weaknesses and fears, all our strengths and gifts, and to allow ourselves to have them, is humility, the inner attitude which brings healing and self-healing. What we are about in working with incest, whether as survivors or helpers, is the constant discovery and celebration of ourselves as we actually and separately are.

I was relatively lucky in that none of my brothers or sisters openly doubted me when I finally told them, by letter, what our father had done to me. Intellectually I had no fears about telling them, but my body perhaps knew better. For I was in the course of typing out the letter to each of them, over a few days, when I was struck down, over the course of the same few days, by an auto-immune disease, sarcoidosis, so badly that I became completely helpless, had to be hospitalised, and did not recover for two months. In auto-immune diseases the body produces antibodies, which attack constituents of its own tissue. It was as if my body was enacting within itself what was happening within my family. Part of my family, me, was attacking the family itself, 'The Family', which had always seemed more important than any one member of it. My action destroyed the notion of 'The Family' for me, made my brothers and sisters emerge as individuals each responding characteristically to the fact which I was presenting to them. There are no accepted guidelines laid down as to how to react to such news, and each brother and sister therefore revealed themselves as they are.

For many survivors, the group becomes more important than their own families. I have often sat listening while survivors recounted, trying to accept the words as they spoke them, how their families reject them, hold them to ridicule, call them crazy, a troublemaker, a liar. It is very threatening to some families that their daughter, sister, niece, is coming to an incest survivors' group. 'You don't want to mix with people like that', Fiona, an incest survivor was told. The hurt of the implied rejection made it hours before the realisation surfaced in Fiona's mind — 'But *I am one of them!*'

Often families try to minimise what has happened, to hush it up, tell the survivor to forget it has ever happened. This denial is not simply the embarrassment that bereaved people often meet with, when people cross the road rather than greet someone who has suffered a loss, though it contains an element of that. But brothers and sisters, children of the same father, who have not been sexually abused, nonetheless carry painful wounds of their own.

155

After all, they are veterans of the same war. There are many ways to avoid confronting their own woundedness, but avoidance becomes impossible if their sister is confronting hers openly. Forgetting it ever happened is the last thing a survivor should try to do, no matter what anyone advises. But though it would be infinitely comforting and affirming to be able to share experiences freely with one's brothers and sisters, it can be less bruising to ourselves to remember in the company of other incest survivors. For it is not necessary to say anything to brothers and sisters. Many survivors castigate themselves needlessly for being too hesitant to speak about incestuous experience. But brothers and sisters can really put us through hell, and sometimes do. It can be common sense, and not cowardice, that prevents us from making ourselves vulnerable. Sometimes we have to accept people the way they are, act accordingly, and make the best of what we *can* share.

On the other hand, if we do discuss the past frankly, we might make the discovery, as I did, that we were not the only victim of the sexual abuse in the family. It was in this manner that I at last came to understand the dumb witness of the painful life that my sister Con has led, not dimly and far back in my mind, as I always had, but with a furious and piercing clarity.

The stress, and the risks to be undertaken in the hope of gaining a more honest relationship with our family, can only be weighed up individually. But it is important not to forget that the ultimate goal is to be able to accept ourselves, which does not have to involve being seen as an acceptable member of our family. This desire, ancient and urgent though it may be, can tip us back into the original and unrewarding role.

It was Janet who finally made me understand what incest does, what it meant, and, in some part of me will continue to mean all my life. She only came to the group for a short time, then tried and failed to kill herself, and did not return.

Her pain was too great for us to support her, as we had no leaders at the time.

It takes great courage to say, as she did, in a room full of incest survivors, 'But I loved my father. He was a good father, apart from sexually abusing me.' I kept very still. What she had said was something I had to hold on to, to place in my mental file on Dad, beside every scrap of evidence about him in my possession. All the stories of my brothers and sisters, glowing recollections of his brilliance, his wit, teaching them chess, taking them on 'mystery tours', the play he produced in the house, using them as actors, the fun of it, the parties, holidays, musical evenings. He was a good father, apart from sexually abusing me.

But also there is the fact of David, whose life has been spent in a psychiatric hospital. Of Con being sent away at sixteen, of young Matthew, suddenly and without telling anyone joining the army, never to live in the family again. Of Justin, whose memory before the age of fifteen is a complete blank. There are the brother and sister who will only speak of marvellous memories.

There is the fact that I lived in terror. There is the fact that I knew my father was the most wonderful man in the world. This is the mental chaos which is the classic outcome of the torture of brainwashing, the appearance of one's torturer alternating between good and bad, marvellous, then hugely threatening, trustworthy, then untrustworthy. This is the real damage of incest, the pain of never being able to accept that someone you loved, looked up to, trusted implicitly, could so casually trample all over you, body and soul, but secretly, and then escape, leaving a false trail of extravagantly generous gestures of fatherhood to conceal the deed.

But this is not the only trail he has left, for if it had been, it would be relatively easy to dismiss the pain which remains, and will always remain. Why is it that even now, when the knowledge of his treachery makes sense of all that was previously senseless, makes understandable what was

157

previously and painfully bewildering, he still clings to me, and will not quite die?

Is it that, after all, very little is clear, that the human soul is infinitely complex? Is it that the books that once belonged to my father, and are now in my possession, speak of a man who was searching, through the profound insights of great thinkers, for a way out of some private dilemma, some secret hell of his own? I think of *The Art of Living* by André Maurois, the pencilled notes in the margin, the words underlined, the pages thumbed, his signature on the dusty flyleaf. Like me, he felt he had to study out of books how to live, to him, as to me, it did not come naturally. And it is this commonness of our struggle, this obvious effort, however enfeebled, towards some kind of comprehension, that leaves me with the residual pain of being unable to completely dismiss him. He existed. And his existence, with all its enigma, is as present in those books on my bookshelf as it is in my life story. He can not be neatly labelled a heartless monster because of the incomprehensibility of his heart.

I gather together all the known facets of my father, attempting to join the ragged edges that will not fit, to reconcile the inconsistencies, not, now, with a child's understanding, but as an adult, becoming free. And in doing this, the awareness settles upon me that he is not to be looked at differently, that he was not a different kind of being, that he was neither the hero nor the ogre of my childhood, but perhaps only a human being, beating blindly about in his distress.

'I was in my own home, cooking myself and my child some food, and I was happy. And I suddenly realised how happy I was, after all I have come through. But the thought troubled me – as if I had no right to be happy, and that if I was happy, something bad would happen to prevent it.' Sarah look around the group questioningly. She had been in the group for a year, had moved from being victim to being survivor, and was beginning to want more, to claim more for herself, part protesting at her own daring, part guilty at feeling better, but also astonished that life can be kind, that she could be kind to herself, that she is now in control of the quality of her life.

Letting go of pain is not easy, when it is the only way we have ever known how to be. We wonder who we will be when we are no longer victims, when we have moved away from the group and no longer even think of ourselves as survivors. What will it be like when the incest in our lives no longer matters, when the memories which can never be erased no longer weigh so much in misery and fear that we cannot bear to live with them? To be ordinary, to find out what it is just to be ordinary, is this not what we have always wanted?

But we have come close to these others, our first friends, the first to know the truth about us and still accept us. With their help we have peeled ourselves painfully, wonderingly and then joyfully away from our old victim identity, we have rehearsed with them the testing of new outside relationships. We are the lucky ones, the survivors who have known amongst ourselves moments that contained love. Some people never know love in all their lives.

We have come to know ourselves a little more, to recognise what may be a permanent vulnerability to losing people that we have grown fond of, so that we get this terrific ache when they go, this strange feeling that we don't exist, that nothing exists, that no matter how alive that special relationship was, the fact that it no longer exists means that it might as well not have happened. That if it hadn't happened we would have been saved a lot of pain. We do not know if this feeling is a remnant from childhood, or if it is a part of the human condition.

And we have to work so hard to wrestle with the fear of abandonment, to trust that the friendship did matter, that it did contribute to our growth, and that we can let go freely, trusting that there are lots of warm, gentle people in the world who will not reject us or take advantage of us, and with whom we can be friends. More and more, outside the group, we find that we do not have to try to be liked, that we are likeable, and that there is no reason why we should ever be lonely again.

To leave the group is to demonstrate that we have begun to trust, to have faith in ourselves, faith in other people, faith in the unknown future. Some of us are happy just to start living, looking for good relationships, satisfying jobs, promotion. To treat ourselves to pretty clothes, entertainment, to learn new sports, take time off and go easy on ourselves, is to continue our healing, and to honour our alikeness to all others in our desire for pleasure and relaxation. Other survivors may want also to gather up all their experience and use it constructively according to their strength. They may wish to campaign for public awareness and legal reform, to start incest phone lines or refuges, to hold conferences to seek out the ways through to these initiatives.

The first conference that I attended with the rest of my group will always stay in my mind. How moving it was to sit in the vast circle of women who cared about incest, once more experiencing the levelling impact of not knowing who in the circle was an incest survivor, and who wasn't. And even more overwhelming than before, there came to us survivors the realisation that we are not different, that we are neither victims nor heroines, and that no matter how hard we have to struggle to rediscover the truth about our dignity, we have done only what we had to do in order to survive, knowing that this was the way, and the only way, to joy.

Participant
(For a little girl, at an Action Against Incest conference)

At first we didn't notice her
as she rolled through the circle we made,
exposing her small wiggling limbs
to our loving gaze.

Somebody's child.

'What a funny meeting!'
she crowed,
completing her journey
and returning the way she had come.

A liberated woman.

Don't you see,
that's the way we want to be,
safe, happy, loved,
playing in the centre of ourselves.

Amongst the talking, puzzling,
silence, tears, risk-taking,
vibes of sheer concern,

she shows us the way.

RELAXATION

Sheet Lightning

After
your finger traces
frown and laughter lines.

161

My tired face lays bare
tensions fused in the storm.
Crossed wires cry
confused in the warm air.

Was joy unbound,
or suffering
offered in our embrace?

Only the yielding smell
of sown fields
left to tell.

It is many years since we moved into this house, and much
has happened to us in those years. I remember our first year
here, and the sense of freedom from the necessity of having
to interact daily with neighbours, for the chief attraction
of our house to me was that, though very small, it was
detached, and surrounded by an extensive garden which
kept me safely separate from the dilemmas of dealing
with my shyness. I remember my husband transforming the
rather dull, symmetrical and flat garden into a place of
utmost beauty and ever-changing surprise. I remember
seeing him carting barrowfuls of earth about, creating little
hills and dells in our garden, moving existing bushes to
more interesting positions and planting saplings, fruit trees,
intriguingly-shaped shrubs, heathers and flowers taken
from our previous garden. All this I watched through
windows, in passing from one room to the other of the
house, for the garden was not my domain, but his. The
place I knew best in the garden was the path leading from
the front door to the gate. I couldn't feel any interest, for
though I could see it was beautiful, it was not mine and had
nothing to do with me. And so for years I enclosed myself
in the heart of all this burgeoning life without ever seeking
it as part of myself, without venturing into it with open
eyes, without ever finding and using it to its limits.

Looking back to those first years now, I see them as incredibly cramped and rigid years for me, years in which I acted as though it was still necessary to maintain a precarious balance on the tightrope I had started to walk as a very small child. Indeed when I met Eve I was still high up there, far removed from anyone, terrified of the fall into the abyss, and determined to keep control over the tiny space where I allowed myself to exist. And it seems to me that what Eve did was to reach up to me, to let me hear her and hold her hand till at last I allowed myself to look at her and discover no abyss, but solid ground beneath me, and a person standing on it, waiting for me to join her. And over the months that followed, the tightrope lowered and lowered until finally it was lying flat on the ground, and all I had to do, to be like everyone else in my own eyes, was to step off it, setting my foot on that ground of reality, and despite total disorientation, learn to walk on it, at the same time developing a sense of direction.

The second part of the process, the learning to walk with confidence, took four times as long as the first part. I couldn't have managed that part alone either. It took that long for me to get to the point where I no longer felt in need of reassurance. But for the whole of that time, reassurance was available to me whenever I needed it. After Eve, came another worker on the clinic staff, who continued the work with equal ease of accuracy, giving me reassurance as a parent. Survivors are always unsure of their abilities as parents, for they have no trustworthy models.

For fifteen months of that time we worked with marriage guidance counsellors, who were also trained in sex therapy and integrated both approaches. This was a particularly healing way to understand our sexual difficulties, as they were not dealt with in isolation from the rest of our relationship, in a mechanical fashion. Their treatment was blended in with ordinary marriage counselling, so that we came to see that making love was one way among many, albeit the most complete way, of expressing all that we felt

163

for each other, and all that we felt about ourselves. We were taught with loving skill how to communicate both verbally and sexually, how to drop our too high expectations, accept reality, each other, ourselves, and value what we had.

And then there were the months spent with the incest survivors' group, watching, listening and sharing, as one after another we opened our lives to each other, daring to trust and continually being rewarded by finding the gain in the loss of that kind of safety we had all been hiding in. The most poignantly moving aspect of being in the group for me, was hearing survivor after survivor express doubt about her right to speak, to be given any kind of hearing, even to be there at all. Each one felt their own extremely painful case to be, for one reason or another, less painful than anyone else in the group. In other words, survivors have to be given special reassurance as to their freedom to express themselves, their long denied right to be listened to and cared for, even sometimes of their right to exist. At the same time we became increasingly aware that we were involved in an adventure, both as individuals and as a group. For many of us, it was our first experience of the power of gentleness. For me, it was as if each time a survivor opened herself to view a little more, she enabled me to enter the places in myself that were still closed. In this way, for instance, the discordant memory of my enormously awe-filled idolisation of my father, existing alongside the fear, was exposed, and with it, the key to the reason I had forgotten for so long the searing humiliation of his treachery.

All this, too, had to be absorbed and accepted, just as the conflicting feelings for my mother had been. All this was slowly worked through in the course of time, a time which I now look back on as a gradual relaxation of tension, the tension of the inner tightrope which had been stretched almost to breaking point. A time which, even at the start was marked by my impatience, as I repeatedly asked Eve, 'Why is it taking so long?', and heard her reply, 'How long has it taken to build up?'. A lifetime. I could not expect instant results. In all, it took over two years for me to begin to learn what the word 'relaxation' means.

In the Oxford English Dictionary, the first definition of the word 'relaxation' is 'partial remission of penalty'. Yes, I can agree with that, from a perspective that the lexicographers could not begin to imagine. Another definition is the word 'recreation'. Re-creation. It was only re-creating my past that enabled me to relax enough to move on from it. To move into finding my own form of recreation, the recreation which is so vital to preserve equilibrium, the balance needed if one is to walk, steadily and aware, through the uncertainty of the reality of a suffering world. In recreation, physical, sexual, sensual, intellectual, I become my own play therapist. I re-create each time in a new form, the surprise of being me.

Over all this time, I have fashioned my own personal definition of relaxation. It has to do with the discovery of feeling. It has to do with expanding my consciousness to the limits of the space that I live in. It has to do with lying in the sun, shaded by weeping willow and quivering aspen leaves, in the garden that I have never until now claimed as my own, though it is mine. Lying still enough to feel my unborn child moving within me, as I know the small goldfish swims in the dark waters of the pool my husband made so long ago.

It has to do with knowing I am going to enjoy this child, even if I am not the perfect mother. It has to do with building faith in my lover, in myself as a lover, in our ability to sustain and develop love. It has to do with the ability to cease struggling, fluttering like a fallen fledgling lifted in the hand of a human. To cease struggling and relax long enough to feel, in that sudden stillness, the constant rhythm of life flowing through my veins, through time and space, work and play, terror and hope, anger and love, through my outer and inner being, continually connecting and disconnecting objective and subjective experience so as to bring them into a simple harmony, the music of the heart's

blood covering and uncovering, concealing and disclosing
the naked shore of the human spirit.

The love of the beach for the ocean

You leave me calm,
retreating slowly to your own place
where your own work
goes on each day. I am alone now
and resting in your wake.
Small tender things shift
in the shallows of my folds, driftwood
where limpets cling, pale pink shells
gleam in the sun, and little boys
run over me, to catch and feel
the frantic hermit crabs
that dodge their footsteps,
and their podgy starfish hands
grab holes in me, for you to heal
when you return.
                  When you return –
what crashing of spray goes on!
How you knock down their castles
and how the tourists run
back to their hotels from sunning themselves
on me, and then, when it is all done,
and you are in our place,
you let me see what life is in you,
cool green fronds, transparent jellyfish,
giant stones and schools of silver dabs,
each in their territorial ponds,
caress the currents that flow strong in you,
until the moment ebbs,
you lovingly retreat, and know,
you leave me calm.

Selected Bibliography

FIRST-PERSON ACCOUNTS

Maya Angelou, *I Know Why the Caged Bird Sings* (autobiography), Virago Press, London, 1983

Louise Armstrong, *Kiss Daddy Goodnight*, Pocket Books, New York, 1978

Ellen Bass and Louise Thornton (eds.), *I Never Told Anyone*, Harper and Row, London, 1983

Toni McNaron and Yarrow Morgan, *Voices in the Night*, Cleis Press, Pittsburg, 1982

Constance Nightingale, *Journey of a Survivor* (poetry); *The Nightingale Roars*: an incest survivor's journey to freedom (video), both available from Constance Nightingale, c/o 37–39 Jamaica Street, Bristol 1, 1986

FICTION

Kitty Fitzgerald, *Marge*, Sheba Feminist Publishers, London, 1984

Michelle Morris, *If I Should Die Before I Wake*, Black Swan, London, 1984

Alice Walker, *The Color Purple*, Women's Press, London, 1983

NON-FICTION BOOKS TO HELP SURVIVORS AND OTHERS

Lynn B. Daugherty, *Why Me?* (help for victims of child sexual abuse even now they are adults), Mother Courage Press, Racine, Wisconsin, 1984

Anne Dickson, *A Woman in Your Own Right* (assertiveness and you), Quartet, London, 1982

Anne Dickson, *The Mirror Within* (your sexuality), Quartet, 1985

Eliana Gil, *Outgrowing the Pain*, Launch Press, San Francisco, 1983

Harold S. Kushner, *When Bad Things Happen to Good People* (a religious perspective on innocent suffering), Pan, London, 1982

Ginny McCarthy, *Getting Free* (leaving abusive relationships), The Seal Press, Seal Beach, California, 1982

Robin Norwood, *Women Who Love Too Much* (for over-nurturing women), Arrow, London, 1986

OTHER NON-FICTION

Sandra Butler, *Conspiracy of Silence: the trauma of incest*, Volcano, San Francisco, 1982

Judith Herman, *Father–Daughter Incest*, Harvard, Cambridge, Mass., 1980

Karen Meiselman, *Incest*, Jossey Bass, San Francisco, 1978

Alice Miller, *Thou Shalt Not Be Aware*, Pluto Press, London, 1985

Alice Miller, *The Drama of Being a Child*, Virago Press, London, 1987

Alice Miller, *For Your Own Good: the roots of violence in child-rearing*, Virago Press, London, 1987

Sarah Nelson, *Incest: Fact and Myth* (an incisive and revealing study, compactly written), Stramullion, Edinburgh, 1982

Pinew and Dare, *Secrets in the Family*, Faber, London, 1978

Florence Rush, *The Best Kept Secret* (historical perspective), Prentice Hall, Englewood Cliff, New Jersey, 1980

Robert Stein, *Incest and Human Love*, Spring Publications, Salisbury, England, 1984

Elizabeth Ward, *Father–Daughter Rape*, Women's Press, London, 1984

D.J. West, *Sexual Victimisation* (results of survey conducted by the Institute of Criminology, University of Cambridge), Gower, Aldershott, England, 1985